Retelling the Biblical Story

Retelling the Biblical Story

H. Stephen Shoemaker

BROADMAN PRESS
Nashville, Tennessee

© Copyright 1985 • Broadman Press
All rights reserved
4221-14
ISBN 0-8054-2114-9

Dewey Decimal Classification: 252
Subject Headings: SERMONS—COLLECTED WORKS // PREACHING
Library of Congress Catalog Card Number: 85-16650
Printed in the United States of America

Unless otherwise noted, all Scripture quotations are taken from the Revised Standard Version of the Bible, copyrighted 1946, 1952, © 1971, 1973.

All Scripture quotations marked KJV are taken from the King James Version of the Bible.

All Scripture quotations marked NEB are taken from *The New English Bible.* Copyright © The Delegates of the Oxford University Press and the Syndics of the Cambridge University Press, 1961, 1970. Reprinted by permission.

All Scripture quotations marked NASB are taken from the *New American Standard Bible.* Copyright © The Lockman Foundation, 1960, 1962, 1963, 1968, 1971, 1972, 1973, 1975, 1977. Used by permission.

All Scripture quotations marked *The Jerusalem Bible* are taken from *The Jerusalem Bible,* copyright 1966 by Darton, Longman and Todd, Ltd. and Doubleday and Company, Inc. Used by permission of the publisher.

Excerpts from RUTH (Anchor Bible) translated and edited by Edward F. Campbell. Copyright © 1975 by Doubleday & Company, Inc. Reprinted by permission of the publisher.

The poem "The Kingdom" by R. S. Thomas is reprinted from *Later Poems* (London: Macmillan, 1984) by permission of Macmillan, London and Basingstoke.

Library of Congress Cataloging-in-Publication Data

Shoemaker, H. Stephen, 1948-
  Retelling the Biblical story.

  1. Bible—Homiletical use. 2. Bible—History of
Biblical events. 3. Story-telling (Christian
theology) 4. Story sermons. I. Title.
BS534.5.S56   1985   251   85-16650
ISBN 0-8054-2114-9

*To my parents
who told me the story of Jesus
and took me to church
where I could hear it over and over again.*

Acknowledgments

A preacher learns to preach from the moment of birth. Where does one begin to pay acknowledgment? The book is dedicated to my parents who told me the story of Jesus and took me to church where I could hear it over and over again. I thank two congregations, Beverly Hills Baptist Church, Asheville, North Carolina, and Crescent Hill Baptist Church, Louisville, Kentucky, who heard these sermons and, in their listening, taught me to listen better and preach better. I thank two contemporary biblical storytellers whose influence is beyond footnoting: Elie Wiesel, master Jewish storyteller, and Frederick Buechner, brilliant novelist and profound Christian preacher.

There are four persons who have helped me in the production of this book: R. Alan Culpepper and Paul D. Duke, who read the manuscript and gave encouragement and advice; Martina Carter and Johnnie Sherwood who typed and retyped the manuscript. Many thanks.

And I want to say thanks to my wife, Cherrie, who keeps encouraging me to tell the Bible stories in my preaching and who embodies the *hesed* of God in our covenant relationship.

Preface

A first book on preaching is not a *summa;* it is an intuition spoken with passion and, hopefully, some light. The basic intuition of this book is captured in two images. The first image is that of T. S. Eliot, who, in *The Rock,* pictured the human heart "shivering and fluttering" between the church and the world, between "heaven gate" and "hell gate." In the preaching event the preacher offers the hearer the biblical world that the hearer "shivering and fluttering" between that world and the world of earth might choose the former and enter "heaven gate."

The second image comes from Martin Buber's *Tales of the Hasidim:*

> I shall teach you the best way to say Torah. You must cease to be aware of yourselves. You must be nothing but an ear which hears what the universe of the word is constantly saying within you. The moment you start hearing what you yourself are saying, you must stop.

In the preaching event the preacher points not to the preacher's world or to the hearer's world but to a third reality which embraces them both, the biblical world. Good preaching is *unselfconscious* preaching. When we preach we seek to hear the Word of God and speak it to God's children. The moment we start hearing ourselves preach, we must stop.

The design of this book provides a collection of sermons which retell the Biblical Story. These sermons are for everybody. In my church the children and youth have enjoyed them as much as the adults. They have the deepest and broadest appeal of all my sermons—not only across age lines but also across social, educational, and theological lines.

This book also provides a theology of narrative preaching. This section is designed for the theological student, the preacher, and the layperson who want to move behind the sermon to see why preachers preach and how they craft their sermons. I put this chapter at the end, but many of you will want to read it first.

After the introduction there is a sermon which tells the whole Biblical Story. Then will come twelve Old Testament narrative sermons based on the lives of the heroes and heroines of our faith. Next will come three New Testament narrative sermons, a parable, an encounter with Christ, and "Revelation: The End of the Story."

H. STEPHEN SHOEMAKER

Contents

Introduction	11
1. The Biblical Story	15
2. Noah	26
3. Jacob	35
4. Joseph	43
5. Moses	50
6. Elijah, 1	59
7. Elijah, 2	68
8. Amos	77
9. Hosea	84
10. Jonah	92
11. Daniel	100
12. Job	108
13. Ruth	117
14. The Rich Man and Lazarus	126
15. Zacchaeus and Jesus: The Day the Camel Passed Through the Needle's Eye	133
16. Revelation: The End of the Story	139
17. The Theology of Narrative Preaching	148

Introduction

"Faith comes from hearing," the apostle Paul said (Rom. 10:17, NASB). Hearing what? Hearing the gospel, the good story, hearing the Biblical Story, the "old, old story of Jesus and his love"; the story of God's Son who became a man and walked this earthly world to give and to show us a love that would never end; the story of a crucified Messiah whose death somehow, some way reconciles us with God.

But the Story also reaches back to creation's dawn where everything that was made was made by the Word of God in the image of this same Christ—"in him, ... through him and for him" (Col. 1:16), the Colossians hymn would sing years, maybe millions of them, after the fact.

And the Story continues to its glorious end when the Christ shall come again, He the Judge with the heart of a Savior who died for me, this time not in suffering love as in the first Advent, but in triumphant love. Then shall come the time when all things shall be reconciled; then shall come the new heaven and new earth, the supper of the Lamb, and "the song of them that triumph, The shout of them that feast."

To hear that Story and to enter it is to experience the birth of faith; it is to have your own salvation story.

All that from hearing? Yes. And such is why we should never stop telling Bible stories, the Biblical Story. The most terrible famine imaginable, said the prophet Amos, is not a famine of meat or grain but a famine of God's Word. "Will Jesus find faith on earth when he returns?" was the ardent question of early Christians. Yes—if we tell the Story. For faith comes by hearing.

This book is a collection of narrative sermons and is also a theology of narrative preaching. The sermons are a retelling of Bible stories. More than that, they are, as the book's title suggests, a retelling of the Biblical Story, the Story of God's way with us and our way with God.

The book arises from the conviction of the primacy of storytelling as a vehicle for the transmission of the gospel. It also arises from a context of the neglect of the biblical narratives in our churches and classrooms today.[1]

As modern rationalists we have presided over what Hans Frei calls "the eclipse of the Biblical narrative."[2] We have dissected the narrative in an attempt to separate "fact" from "myth," keeping the "truths" and casting aside their story home. We have discarded the story and grabbed for the moral of the story. What we have ended up with are moral points or theological principles, all pale shadows of the truth which the truthful stories themselves convey. It has been a treacherous course, for it is the story itself that conveys not only the moral of the story but also the story's power to transform our lives.

Sunday School lessons are apt to forget the Bible stories and emphasize the "main ideas" of the text. Sermons are apt to discard quickly the story and preach its three or four "points." But such enlightened enterprise has backfired. It denies that we live by more than bread—by stories. More than homo-sapiens or homo-erectus, call us homo-narratus: we tell stories.[3]

Soap operas are popular in our story-starved age because they involve us in an ongoing story. *Roots* set Americans off on a binge of discovering our family stories. Genealogies tell us to some degree who we are. More important, however, than family trees are those mirrors of identity we call Bible stories. When an ancient Hebrew was asked who God was, he started with a story: "My father was a wandering Aramean; his children wound up as slaves in Egypt. But God heard their cries and delivered them from

Pharaoh's grip." When a Christian is asked about God, she begins: "For God so loved the world that he gave his only Son" (John 3:16).

The Bible stories tell us who God is and who we are. To be sure, we see these mirrors of identity "through a glass darkly." We never see God face to face or even perfectly see our own faces. However, in these stories we see enough to be changed. They move us to enter into God's Story and "strike a covenant," to use the language of the Old Testament. When this happens, the truth of the Bible becomes "saving knowledge," for we enter into personal relationship with God and are swept up in the living stream of God's love and power. Then God's Story becomes our salvation story with roots far deeper than our own personal or family stories could ever provide.

So hear the call, Sunday School teachers! Go up into the attic of your church and bring down the old flannel boards! And preachers, do not be afraid to *tell* the stories in your preaching. Tell them as vividly as you can; then trust them to work their holy power in you and in the lives of God's people entrusted to you.

Come let me tell you a story.

Notes

1. The last few years have shown an extraordinary resurgence among scholars and preachers in narrative theology and preaching. This book will give evidence to this new movement. It is none too soon for our story-starved age.

2. Hans Frei, *The Eclipse of the Biblical Narrative* (New York: Harper & Row, 1966). Frei documents that since the Enlightenment we have given up a precritical, "realistic" reading of the text in which we assume the narratives to be the true depictions of reality by which our lives are to be judged. Instead we have been taught to stand as judges over the narratives, sorting out truth (what happened historically) from meaning (what is the moral of the story). It was a deadly decision to have to make, one that never occurred to the original authors and audiences. Our mania to detach the moral or truth of the story from the story itself has been a defensive reaction to those who charged that unless the narratives are "pure history" (whatever that is) they are not true. But we do not have to have given up so much. R. Alan Culpepper's brilliant work *Anato-*

my of the Fourth Gospel: A Study in Literary Design (Philadelphia: Fortress Press, 1983) points us toward a new way of looking at the narrative world of the Bible. He calls biblical narrative—in particular the Gospel of John—"a story of history interpreted by faith" (p. 232). The debate about the relationship between story and history will be noted below. Steven Crites (see note 4, p. 175) also argues that modern society has tried to destroy the narrative character of our experience, by abstraction and contraction, all to our poverty.

3. Northrup Frye, *The Great Code: The Bible and Literature* (London: Ark Paperbacks, 1983), says, "Man lives, not directly or nakedly in nature like the animals, but within a mythological universe, a body of assumptions and beliefs developed from his existential concerns" (p. xvi). Jesus was suggesting the same when he told the Tempter, "Man [does] not live by bread alone but by every word that proceeds from the mouth of God" (Matt. 4:4).

1
The Biblical Story

What I attempt in this chapter is preposterous: a retelling of the Biblical Story in a few pages. Such an enterprise is dangerous because such a compression of biblical material must be almost absurdly selective, and the selection process may reveal more about the preacher than about God. But it is based on two vital assumptions.

The first assumption is that, as Paul said, "Faith comes by hearing"—hearing the Biblical Story—and, however badly it is told, God has the power to bless the telling by opening the ears of the hearers so they come to faith and enter the Story themselves.

The second assumption is that the Bible's table of contents, the order and selection of all the sixty-six books, is a revelation of God. The table of contents tells us that God is a world-making, history-making, story-making God and we His creation and His creatures are His story. Look how the Bible is put together. It is not a set of lectures; nor is it a logical set of precepts set down in proper order. It is a story with a beginning, a dynamic plot, and an end toward which all reality is moving.

Therefore, this outrageous Reader's Digest condensation is both possible and necessary; it is possible because the broad plot of the Biblical Story is a revelation itself, and it is necessary lest we miss the story for all the historical details and scholarly footnotes—missing the forest for the trees.

Hear now the Story.

Creation

The Biblical Story begins at the dawn of creation. "In the beginning *GOD*." Before anything else was, God was. "In the beginning God *created*," created the heavens and the earth. God spoke and life came forth from nothingness; God spoke and cosmos was formed out of chaos.

The creation account is bold to announce that God liked what He had made and called it *good*. Creation was the good act of a good God. Genesis wages war with all the myths of its time. Creation was not the result of bloody war between gods; it was the free act of the one true and good God. It wages war against the gnostic myth that an evil God created an evil, material world. It wages war against any atheistic myth of creation that suggests that creation was the random act of blind molecules and history is the theater of the absurd. Creation is the purposeful, good act of God.

But the creation account is bolder still. It says that the human race is the crown of God's creation, the glorious climactic work of the sixth day. It is as if the universe was made for *us*. God made for us a garden of a home on a jeweled planet and placed us in it.

That is how the Biblical Story begins—with the astonishing notion that this vast universe is the creation of a good God and that God gave us this world saying, "Here is your home. It has all you need to flourish as my children. Take good care of it. It is made for you." The implications of all of this are staggering: creation is to be enjoyed, not despised or destroyed; and since God has given it to us we must take responsibility for it with Him.

Fall and Covenant

The Story tells of an early relationship with God that was communion full and free. The One who shaped us, who made us in His own image and blew into us His breath, walked with us in the cool of the day.

Then comes that story of the fall. The story of the fall is not just about one man and woman; it is about us all. It tells of one man and woman who fell, and it tells of the way we all tend to fall.

A suggestion came to Eve's heart, delivered by a serpent, that

God did not have our best interests at heart, that His rules were not fair, that they were given to keep us from gaining equality with Him. We can be like God, we were told; just eat the forbidden fruit of the tree of the knowledge of good and evil. Adam and Eve jumped at the chance, disobeyed God, and ate the "apple." So began the fall, but it was far from over. It is the tumble all of us take.

The fruit stands in every age as the temptation to be like God, to know everything, and to be able to do anything—in short, to be done with this rule-making God.

From the original peace of the garden we call Eden came the wilderness of warfare, the age of discord, division, distrust, and disease, the age of anxiety, estrangement, and apartheid. What God had brought together we tore asunder. What He created we turned back to chaos. And we ran and hid, naked.

At this point God could have given up on His creation. But He did not. He decided to commit Himself to us no matter what. He decided to remain faithful to His creation and to us, His human creatures, even though we did not stay faithful to Him. He determined in His heart to do whatever He had to do, to give whatever He had to give in order that His creation might flourish. He could have turned His back, but He did not. The way the Hebrew people expressed it was in their favorite verse, the John 3:16 of the Old Testament, Exodus 34:6: "The Lord, a God merciful and gracious, slow to anger, abounding in steadfast love and faithfulness."

And the word they used to describe this character of God was *hesed,* the faithful loving-kindness of God, the steadfast, stubborn, patient, never-giving-up, no-matter-what love of God.

God showed His faithfulness not only in creation but also in covenant, as He entered into our lives and said, "I will be your God, if you will be my people." He made a covenant with Noah after He saved him and all humankind from the Flood. And He made a covenant with Abraham and his descendants, the Hebrew people, not just for his sake and theirs but so that through him "all the families of the earth shall be blessed" (Gen. 12:3, NASB).

Exodus and Torah

The most dramatic revelation of God's faithful loving-kindness was through the Exodus, the deliverance of the Hebrew people from slavery in Egypt. God wants none of His children living in the yoke of slavery, so He is eternally, forever historically at work to free the oppressed and to crush the oppressor, to open the door of every prison so that every person might flourish.

The next way He revealed His love was through the Torah, through the living Law of God that teaches us how to live fully and freely. It is no accident that the Exodus and the Torah go together. On Mount Sinai God said, "I am the God who set you free from Pharaoh; now I will teach you how to *stay* free" (see Ex. 20:2).

> Thou shalt have no other gods before me.
> Thou shalt not make . . . any graven image.
> Thou shalt not take the name of the Lord thy God
>   in vain.
> Remember the sabbath day to keep it holy.
> Honour thy father and thy mother.
> Thou shalt not kill.
> Thou shalt not commit adultery.
> Thou shalt not steal.
> Thou shalt not bear false witness.
> Thou shalt not covet (Ex. 20:3-4,7-8,12-17, KJV).

The story goes that the people accepted the Ten Commandments. Rabbi Abraham Heschel reasoned:

> Man had to be expelled from the Garden of Eden;
>   he had to witness the murder of half of the
>   human species by Cain;
>   experience the catastrophe of the Flood;
>   the confusion of the languages;
>   slavery in Egypt
>   and the wonder of the Exodus,
> to be ready to accept the law.[1]

But the acceptance did not last long. We would not keep the Torah. We called it new slavery and ran from it. Priests did not help; they expanded the Ten Commandments into 613, 365 negative ones for the days of the year, and 248 positive ones for the number of bones in a man's body. Neither saint nor CPA could keep count. The Torah was trivialized by some, made into a prison by others, domesticated by some, ignored by the rest.

Prophecy

So God in His faithfulness sent prophets to us. Prophets reminded us of the original intent of the Law. Micah cut through the tangle of 613 rules and gave us the great prophetic summary: This is what God requires—"To do justice, and to love kindness and to walk humbly with your God" (Mic. 6:8). The prophets were sent to rebuke kings and priests who presided over God's Law and perverted it by using it for their own purposes. They were sent to warn of imminent judgment for the nation unless the nation turned back to God and learned to love the Torah again.

The prophets' hearts burned with the Word of God, and they dreamed God's vision of a day when the Word of God would cover the earth as the waters that cover the earth, of a day when the Law of God would be written on the fleshly tablets of our hearts, when swords would be beat into plowshares and we would learn war no more. But the prophets were beaten, jailed and killed, forgotten, and remembered only by a few disciples who hid their words in their hearts.

What followed the age of prophecy was the dark age of God's silence. One writer spoke of times of God's silence. They are times of judgment. We have so misused His name and distorted His word that, for a time, God stops speaking so that we can learn again to tell the difference between the sound of His voice and ours. He asks: "Could it be that in order to judge the misuse of his name within the church, God reveals himself by creating silence about himself?" Is God's silence "God's way of forcing his church back to a sacred embarrassment when speaking of him?"[2]

Such a time, so history tells us, was that time between the Testaments, the last few centuries BC. The thought was widespread in the Judaism of that day that God had stopped speaking, that the Spirit had withdrawn. The age of prophecy was over. All they had to rely on was the past revelation of Law and Prophets.

All you could hear now, they said, was what they called the *batqol*, the daughter of the voice, a faint echo of the Word. For example, it was said of the great first-century (BC) rabbi Hillel, "He was so good he would have been a prophet had prophecy not ceased." Such was the darkness of the age after the prophets. And most became well accustomed to the dark. What began as the judgment of God became for them the perfectly normal "way things were."

Gospel

Then a miracle happened—*the* miracle. In Ignatius' words: "Jesus Christ, his son, who is his word proceeding from silence." John, in his Gospel, said that the Word of God through whom the world was made "became flesh and dwelt among us, full of grace and truth" (John 1:14).

The Spirit of God had returned! The same Spirit that moved across the face of the deep and created heaven and earth moved across the life of a young teenager named Mary; and she bore a Son of heaven and earth whose name was Jesus, which meant "God will save his people."

The Divine Word did not just seize this man Jesus as God's Word seized prophets of old. The Divine Word *was* Jesus. The good news, the gospel, the good story was that the *hesed* love of God, His faithful loving-kindness, his determination to make a success of His creation, His commitment to do all He could do and give all He could give in order for His creatures to flourish, this *hesed* love became flesh in Jesus of Nazareth.

This man Jesus lived in the immediacy of God's loving care. He called God Abba, Father, Daddy, and invited *us* to do the same.

He preached the kingdom of God, not as some distant hope, but as an immediate, urgent, compelling, gracious possibility. "The kingdom of God is *among* you," Jesus said [*entos* you, in Greek], within you, in your midst. Scholars argue over the exact translation, but we dare not submerge the startling and audacious message in scholastic squabble. Whatever it means, it means that the kingdom of God is *here*, not there; *near*, not far; here whether you like it or not, available whether you choose it or not.

Because the kingdom of God was the kingdom of *God,* it was

The Biblical Story

best taught by Jesus in parables. Jesus told hundreds of them, of a father running to welcome home a prodigal son, of the first becoming last and the last first, of lost coins being found, of good neighbors, foolish virgins, and joyous wedding feasts, of choices that had to be made, the either/or of the kingdom of God which means life and death. R. S. Thomas, contemporary Welsh poet, writes of "The Kingdom":

> It's a long way off but inside it
> There are quite different things going on:
> Festivals at which the poor man
> Is king and the consumptive is
> Healed; mirrors in which the blind look
> At themselves and love looks at them
> Back; and industry is for mending
> The bent bones and the minds fractured
> By life. It's a long way off, but to get
> There takes no time and admission
> Is free, if you will purge yourself
> Of desire, and present yourself with
> Your need only and the simple offering
> Of your faith, green as a leaf.[3]

Jesus, however, not only taught the Kingdom. Full of the power of the Spirit, He brought it near in His life. It came near in the way He healed the sick, opened blind eyes, and set free those in chains. It came near in His simple friendship with tax collectors and sinners, with outcasts, women, and children. When He ate and drank with them, the Kingdom came near in joy. He was comfort to the weary, welcome to the despised, Savior to all who wandered lost in the earth.

He was One whom people never forgot, whose face they could not escape. Maybe the reason was the compassion of His words, "Come to Me, all who are weary and heavy-laden" (Matt. 11:28, NASB). Maybe it was the kindness of His eyes, or the authority of His voice. When He said, "your sins are forgiven" you knew they were; they fell like dead scales from your skin, fell like weights from your shoulders, fell like tears from your heart. Surely it was in the way He died. You might have guessed even had you not already heard. A tumbling and fallen world would not welcome such a one as He. Religious authorities hated Him because His authority made theirs sound screeching and empty. Political authorities feared Him because without His ever saying it, they knew He was King and no king wants another greater around. So they conspired to kill Him, Jerusalem and Rome, priest and politician; and the mob, wanting easy answers and quick solutions, went drunkenly along.

So they put Him to death, made Him a public spectacle, poked Him up a hill, pressed into His skull a crown of thorns, mocked Him with a sign above his dying head that read "King of the Jews." Only a few heard Him cry through parched lips, "Father, forgive them for they know not what they do" (Luke 23:34). And as He died, the world held its breath, or should have. We had crucified the only Son of God.

The darkness of our *NO* to God lasted until the third day after His death. Then came Easter morning when God raised Jesus from the dead. It was the trumpet call of the victory of life over death, of love over all the hate we could muster. It was a sign of a love that will not let us go. God raised Jesus from the dead to say to all who would see that God has won the victory over the powers of darkness and death.

It was the sign of God's *hesed,* His faithful loving-kindness. The New Testament found its own way to capture the meaning of the event, the gospel of Jesus Christ, His life, death, and resurrection: "For God so loved the world that he gave his only Son that whoever believes in him should not perish but have eternal life" (John 3:16). The apostle Paul said, "But God shows his love for us in that while we were yet sinners Christ died for us" (Rom. 5:8).

And the New Testament found its own word for God's *hesed,* the gospel come in Jesus. *Grace* they called it, the free gift of salvation, the inconceivable mercy, the unstoppable love, Jesus the Christ: "He is surprise of Mercy, outgoing Gladness, Rescue, Healing and Life."[4]

Church

The God who did not abandon us on the cross as we had abandoned Him created the church as the ongoing incarnation of Christ, His body. On Pentecost Day the Spirit that moved across

The Biblical Story

the face of the deep and created the heavens and earth, that overshadowed Mary's flesh and brought forth Jesus, that descended upon Jesus at His baptism and empowered His earthly ministry, this same Spirit descended upon the church. And people amid tongues as of fire discovered that they were made out of many peoples one people, out of many tongues one tongue, "for in Christ there is neither Jew nor Gentile, male nor female, master nor slave" (see Gal. 3:28).

The church was the miracle creation of God, a royal priesthood, a holy nation, for, "Once you were no people, but now you are God's people; once you had not received mercy, but now you have received mercy" (1 Pet. 2:10).

The church became the body of Christ, a community of peace and grace, fashioned by God to tell His good news and to incarnate the love of Christ to all people for all time.

The story of the church is a mixture of shadow and light, faith and unfaith, discipleship and denial. We have taken on not only Peter's confession "Thou art the Christ," but also his impulsive and unpredictable nature—one moment a rock of faith, the next a series of shabby denials. The church has been the object of much praise and scorn throughout our history, but in truth we have been both far better and far worse than our critics know us to be. By the mystery of God's grace, we have been Christ's face to the world, His hands, feet, and heart. And we have also been Christ's betrayer, an Antichrist, a mockery of His name and face. But God in His faithfulness has been sure on His promise to accompany us with the living spirit of Christ, and that has resulted in the true church being somewhere in all places and times of our history.

Apocalypse

What is left? The Bible does not leave us with the halting step and faltering voice of the church. We are told the end of the Story. Given a vision by angels, John on the Isle of Patmos delivered to us the Book of Revelation. It pictures history as a fight to the finish between the forces of good led by the Holy Trinity—God the Father, Son, and Spirit—and the forces of evil led by the unholy trinity of the dragon, the beast, and the false prophet. The powers of darkness rage until the last moment of history—which is warning against the illusion that we will bring in the perfect kingdom by our power. However, the Book of Revelation, written during a time of great persecution, is God's word of assurance to us all. God will win the final victory—regardless of how it looks at times. In the end the battle will go to the good and we, stripped of all costumes and masks, will be known by our true faces.

Christ shall come again, this time not in suffering love as in the first Advent, but in triumphant love.

The Story pictures the last judgment, but we who know Christ should not fear. The great medieval cathedral art pictures why. In the judgment scene the judge is Christ, His hands raised so that we can see His scars. The message is clear. The One coming to judge is the same as the One who died for us. There will be perfect justice and even more perfect mercy.

The Story pictures the end of time. There shall be a new heaven and a new earth, a new Eden, a home where we will dwell with God and He with us, where He will wipe away every tear, and death will be no more. Now we see only through a glass darkly, said Paul; but then we will see face to face and understand as we are now understood. Then truth and love will wed and we will gather around the supper of the Lamb; then shall be "The song of them that triumph, The shout of them that feast" ("Jerusalem the Golden").

That is the Biblical Story; it spans all the past, present, and future. It is God's Story. It can be yours. I invite you to enter it. If you refuse, all the false stories of our age will hold their sway; you will dwell in the enthralling kingdoms of this world that promise life but only give death. But if you enter the Biblical Story, you will know God as your Father, you will know Jesus as Savior, Lord, and Friend; you will have more brothers and sisters, mothers and fathers than history can contain; and you will have a story, a salvation story, and so live in the living stream of God's love and power.

Hear, enter, and live.

Notes

1. Abraham Heschel, *I Asked for Wonder: A Spiritual Anthology*, ed. Samuel H. Dresner (New York: Crossroad, 1983), p. 91.
2. Cited in James A. Sanders, *God Has a Story Too* (Philadelphia: Fortress Press, 1979), p. 77.
3. R. S. Thomas, *Later Poems* (London: Macmillan, 1984), p. 35. Reprinted by permission of Macmillan, London and Basingstoke.
4. George A. Buttrick, *Prayer* (New York: Abingdon, 1942), p. 83.

2
Noah

It is unfortunate that we have turned Noah's flood into a fairy tale for children. It is packaged as just another "Golden Book" on the shelf beside "Jack and the Beanstalk." Or it is made into a plastic toy: Noah's ark complete with ark, Noah and his family, and two each of an assortment of animals. You can find it somewhere between Fisher-Price's barnyard set and the Star Wars collection.

It in fact is a story of deepest truth and meaning, as full of darkness and light as any of us can handle—child or adult. It has to do with age-old questions such as: Will God ever get so angry at us because of our sins that He will destroy us? Does God ever use the realm of nature to punish us? Is there a rhyme and reason to our universe? How are we then to live? So it is not *for children only*. It is a story meant for all the people of God.

This story is first and foremost a story about God. The main drama is not what happened on the ark but rather what was going on in the heart of God.

The beginning is dark and ominous. How terrible to see what has become of God's fair creation. God created us in love and called us "good." He commanded us to be fruitful and multiply and to take dominion over all the earth. But Adam and Eve disobeyed God's command. Then Cain murdered Abel and the descent into darkness deepened until our story begins with the words: "The Lord saw that the wickedness of man was great in earth" (Gen. 6:5 a). The narrative does not give all the sordid details, but it does go on to say that the imagination of our hearts was continually evil (v. 5 b) and that the earth was filled with violence (v. 11).

How was God to respond to the pervasive wickedness of His human family? He created us and gave us everything we needed. He gave us proper instructions, then set us free—as love must—to do as we chose to do. Love must set us free, for neither love nor companionship can be coerced. And we, living in the realm of God's freedom, took His gifts and turned them into wickedness, evil, and violence.

How did God respond? Not as an angry tyrant, but as a grieving parent. The story says, "And the Lord was sorry that he had made man on the earth, and it grieved him to his heart" (v. 6). One cannot be a parent without knowing this kind of grief. The word for *grieving* used here to describe God is the same word used to describe the pain of motherhood in Genesis 3:16: "in pain you shall bring forth children." It is a pain beyond that of labor pains; it is the pain of parenthood. One cannot be a parent without pain, for one cannot love without giving freedom and one cannot give freedom without the terrible pain of watching helplessly as your children say no to you, or watching them make mistakes, or watching them get worked over by the world.

So the story describes God. When He saw His beloved creation become disobedient and suffer at its own hands, He did not react like an angry tyrant, but rather as a grieving parent.

His first solution for this pain was to turn His back on His creation, to forget His creatures, to walk away from the world He had made. When one of us turns away from another, isolation is the result. But when God forgets us and turns His back on us, it means extinction. Why? Our lives are held in His hands. As the historian Butterfield put it: "If God stopped breathing we would all vanish." The paths of the planets in the cosmos follow the beat of His heart. All our natural laws are but filiment of light in His hands. I think it was Chesterton who said: "The sun rises not by natural law but because God says, Get up and do it again." We are here because God turned and spoke His Word. If He turns away and stops speaking we then vanish.

What the story tells us is that God, the grieving parent, despaired of His creation. He wished he had never created us. So what He decided was to unmake us. He would take back His creative word and return us to the chaos from which He had brought us. He decided to erase the third day of creation. Remember? On the third day God spoke and the waters that covered the earth separated, the land appeared, and life began on earth. What our weeping, grieving parent of a God did was to turn His back and let the watery chaos submerge the earth again. God grieved that He had ever made us and in His grief He was content that we return to the nothingness from which we had come.

Do you not think God could do that? Do you not believe our every breath is held in His eternity? God despaired of having made us and decided to allow the chaos to consume the world again. Was that not less painful than the pain and violence we were inflicting on each other every day of the week, every hour of the day, with every beat of our hearts?

So God decided to blot us out, to destroy us, to release the watery chaos He had been holding back by his merciful hand and to let the waters cover the earth. "For I am sorry that I have made them" (v. 7), said our God.

But now enters Noah. The text says, "But Noah found favor in the eyes of the Lord" (v. 8). There was one whom God could not forget.

One man, one man only turned the tide of the history of humankind. One person's life is enough to change the world. Noah was the man of that hour. He was, to quote the Scripture, "righteous," he was "blameless," and he "walked with God" (v. 9).

God does some of His best work with individuals. Where there is one righteous person, there is hope. Do you not see, then, the importance of your life? You, one person, can make a difference. The world around you may seem headed toward destruction; but where there is one person, one faithful person, one man or woman

Noah

who still loves God, there is hope. Sometimes our best hope, our highest calling, is not to change the world but simply to stay faithful. God needs only one faithful person. That is our first calling: to stay faithful.

Noah was a righteous man and because there was one such as he who walked with God, the story which up to now darkens in judgment takes a new turn—and with it so does the history of the world. Noah is the embodiment of a new possibility. In him there is the possibility of a new humanity.

The grieving God decided to save His lost world. And He turned to Noah to begin a new humanity. He decided not to end all life on this earth. He spoke a message to Noah that must have bewildered that man—no matter how righteous he was or how closely he walked with God.

God said, "Noah, because the earth is filled with violence, I am allowing the waters to cover the earth once again. However, I have also decided to make a new start with you: a new covenant with you and your descendants. Here is the first part of the plan. Start now building an ark. Here are the blueprints: 300 cubits by 50 cubits by 30 cubits. When it begins to rain, gather two each, male and female, of every kind of animal; then gather your own family into the ark" (see vv. 13-21).

The Scriptures record that "Noah did this; he did all that God commanded" (v. 22). You can imagine the sight of Noah building that ark in his backyard—how he became the laughingstock of the neighborhood. The home owners association complained that this monstrosity of a boat was ruining the real estate values of the neighborhood.

And we have no assurance that even Noah's family went along easily with the plan. To begin with, anyone as righteous and blameless as Noah was probably pretty hard to live with. Then this crazy scheme about a flood and this monstrosity of a boat in the backyard! A religious fanatic, this Noah. Had he gone off the deep end?

Later Scripture comments that none of the citizens around Noah took the ark as a sign of repentance; they just went on as usual eating, drinking, and working. Even when the rains began they took no concern, or even when the sewers began to back up.

"It's just the Metropolitan Sewer District up to their tricks," they said, "the flood gates have locked up again." So they went on eating, drinking, and complaining about the "ungodly weather," blaming the Metropolitan Sewer District; but it was to no avail, for the rains did not stop. Meanwhile Noah gathered the animals, his family, and provisions into the ark. Soon the ark began to creak and groan; then the water lifted it off the ground.

For forty days and nights it rained, the waters covered the earth, and the only hope of the world was the motley collection in the ark. It couldn't have been an easy voyage. The old joke probably holds true: If it were not for the storm outside, the stench inside would have been unbearable. *Would this rain ever end,* they must have asked themselves, day after day.

At the end of the forty days Noah opened a window and sent forth a raven which went back and forth waiting for the waters to subside. Then he sent a dove to see whether there was any dry land. The dove could not find dry land and returned. Then Noah waited seven days and sent the dove out again. This time the dove returned with a sprig of olive branch in her mouth. How they must have rejoiced at this sign of hope. The waters were receding! Soon they felt the boat scraping the ground, then settling its weight on the craggy terrain of Mount Ararat. Noah opened the window and saw his salvation: All the earth was dry. How had this salvation happened? The text says, "But God remembered Noah and all the beasts and all the cattle that were with him in the ark" (8:1). God remembered. In His remembrance of us is hope of salvation.

"Then God said to Noah, go forth, you and your family and all the animals" (see vv. 15-17).

They went forth. Noah built an altar and there, knee deep in the mud, they knelt and gave thanks to God.

Then the Lord made a promise: "*Never again,*" he said, "never again will I curse my creation because of their evil hearts. Never again will I forget my creation. I promise to you the constancy of nature, the regular rhythm of seedtime and harvest, cold and heat, summer and winter, day and night. As my love shall never cease neither shall these. The constancy of nature will be an enduring sign of my faithful loving-kindness" (see vv. 22-23).

We see again into the heart of God. Our Heavenly Father vowed never again to give up on us. His parent's heart would be filled with infinite patience, long-suffering love. It was like the glimpse into His heart that Hosea saw when he heard God say: "How can I give you up O Ephraim! How can I hand you over, O Israel! . . . My heart recoils within me, my compassion grows warm and tender. I will not execute my fierce anger, . . . for I am God and not man, the Holy One in your midst and I will not come to destroy" (Hos. 11:8-9).

Then our God with the heart of tender compassion made a new covenant with Noah. It was a renewal of the covenant made at creation's dawn with Adam and Eve. A new beginning. He recommissioned them to their original calling: to be faithful and multiply and to take care of the earth. But then He added a new dimension to the covenant. Remember how the wickedness of humankind had caused violence over the face of the earth? Because God had seen this violence He issued a new dimension of the covenant: It was to be a covenant of *peace*. It was peace between God and humankind: The warfare was over between us. It was also a covenant of peace among all persons. We are not just to have dominion over the animals; we are now to be our brother and sister's keeper. There is to be no violence and bloodshed. "Whoever sheds the blood of man, by man shall his blood be shed; for God made man in his own image" (9:6). The image of God in each of us issues into a reverence for human life—all human life.

God strikes His new covenant with us, a covenant of peace. But it is also a covenant of mercy. God was not deceived. He knew our hearts were still inclined to evil. So out of His unending mercy God said, "*Never again* will I allow the waters to cover the earth. *Never again* will I set out to destroy you. *Never again*. And as a sign of my peace with you, God said, I set this bow in the skies. A bow of colors, a rainbow. The rains will come again, but they will always stop and when they stop you will see this sign of peace, a bow set in the skies" (see vv. 11-17).

God's word is startling. What was this bow set in the skies? The word *bow* is the same word for a warrior's bow.[1] God was saying, "I take my warrior's bow and restring it with all the colors of creation. The warfare is ended; this sign of war I turn into a sign of peace." To use the language of our day, God "unilaterally disarmed" Himself. He dismantled His warheads. God vowed never to destroy us, who so little deserve mercy. That is why His covenant of peace was a sign of unending mercy.

Doesn't this story have real pastoral concern for us? Often when tragedy strikes what sweeps over us and through us is a primeval fear: Is God punishing me? Have I made God angry? What did I do to bring this on? But hear God's promise: Never again. I set before you a covenant of peace. I lay my weapon down.

This does not deny the presence of pain and suffering. It is not to say that our sin does not bring pain and suffering to ourselves and others. There is evil and suffering in this world that God allows because in His love he must set us free, free even to destroy ourselves. Death and destruction are part of our sphere of freedom. We have a terrible and real freedom to destroy this world God has made.

However, hear clearly, death and destruction, pain, evil, and suffering are not rooted in God's anger and rejection. God has determined in His heart not to operate according to the laws of retribution, but according to His inconceivable mercy. What we get from God is not what we deserve, but what we could never earn, the free gift of salvation. The covenant of peace is therefore a covenant of grace.

This story also has real ethical concern. Our discovery that every person is created in God's image changes the way we relate. If God has disarmed Himself, should we not withdraw the weapons we use daily against one another? Is not God a God of peace? Are we not then a people of peace?

While this story cannot be applied directly into the realm of international politics (that is, we cannot use this story to justify unilateral disarmament and tomorrow turn our warheads to rainbows), it should give us undeniable principles with which to live in such an age as ours: the principle of the sacredness of all human life, the warning that we who live by the sword and blood vengeance will die by it, and the moral prohibition against the use of weapons that will do what God has vowed never to do—destroy the world and all He had made. If we children of the ark cannot earnestly and intelligently work for peace, who can?

Hear the new covenant of God with us: "I set my bow in the cloud, and it shall be a sign of the covenant between me and the earth" (v. 13).

This covenant was not lost to the memories of the Hebrew people. As exiles in Babylonian captivity they remembered it and heard God again offering His covenant of peace and saying,

"Fear not, for I have redeemed you. I have called you by name, you are mine. When you pass through the rivers, they shall not overwhelm you. . . . For the mountains may depart and the hills be removed, but my steadfast love shall not depart from you and my covenant of peace shall not be removed" (Isa. 43:1-2; 54:10).

We saw that new covenant in the face of Jesus as He lived among us and heard it on the cross when He said, "Father, forgive them." And we experienced its sure victory as God raised Jesus from the dead and defeated all powers of darkness and death. And we people of God have experienced it time and time again as we have traveled through waters that threatened to engulf us but have been brought through, not by our goodness or strength, but by God's power and mercy. It is in fervent remembrance of God's promise to Noah that we sing our "Crescent Hill Hymn." It is our hymn from the ark. It is our song of confidence in the power and mercy of God.

So let us join with Noah at the altar and give thanks for the new covenant of peace and mercy and hope. Alleluia, Amen.

> We, O God, unite our voices,
> Raised in thankful praise to Thee.
> Thou, unchanging, safe hath brought us
> Through the ever-changing sea.
> Days of calm and days of conflict,
> Nights of darkness prove Thy grace.
> Hands beneath us, arms around us,
> And, above, Thy shining face.
>
> Seeing then the task before us
> Bind our hearts and hands as one.
> May our labor be in union,
> Our resolve and Thine be one.

With one spirit let us labor
Toward the bright horizon far.
In the midst of tempest peril
Be Thy cross our guiding star.

Not our choice the wind's direction,
Unforeseen the calm or gale.
Thy great ocean swells before us,
And our ship seems small and frail.
Fierce and gleaming is Thy myst'ry
Drawing us to shores unknown:
Plunge us on with hope and courage
'Til Thy Harbor is our home! Amen.[2]

Notes

1. Gerhard Von Rad, *Genesis* (Philadelphia: The Westminster Press, 1961), p. 134.
2. The Crescent Hill Hymn, "We, O God, Unite Our Voices," written by Grady Nutt and Paul Duke, sung to the tune HYFRYDOL.

3
Jacob

Jacob sat on the bank of the Jabbok River, all alone, pondering the past and the future. Called by McCartney "the best and the worst man in the Old Testament,"[1] Jacob personifies the struggle all of us have: the struggle between our best self and our worst self, between honesty and deceit. It is the struggle between the faith that receives grace and the unfaith that bargains for grace. Jacob's story is the "Divine Comedy" of a con artist who became the father of the twelve tribes of Israel.

As Jacob sat on the riverbank, he was filled with confusion and dread. And why not? He was returning to meet Esau whom he had cheated out of birthright and blessing, and he had just found out that Esau was coming to meet him with four hundred men. This night might be his last time to look up at the stars. But even the stars gave him no delight. What a mess he had made of his life! It all loomed before him; his life flashed before his eyes that night as he sat on the bank of the Jabbok.

Jacob was a twin, but was born second—Esau first, Jacob second. But as his mother, Rebekah, had told him, Jacob arrived clutching the heel of his brother. So he was named "Jacob," which literally means "foot holder." But to hold someone by the heel is also to trip him up, to supplant him; and this symbolic meaning of the name was to become history.

Jacob didn't remember being born clutching Esau's heel, but he remembered all too well that his father Isaac preferred Esau. Perhaps that was one of the reasons that Rebekah, his mother, preferred Jacob. Each favored by one parent, the boys could not have been more different. Esau: rough, rugged, red-haired, the hunter. Jacob, the homebody, mamma's boy, clever and introspective.

Jacob, sitting on Jabbok's bank, wondered what Esau had in store for him after twenty years. Had Esau forgiven and forgotten? Esau had sworn to kill him, and he had his reasons.

Esau, as the firstborn, was entitled to special spiritual and material benefits from his father. Jacob was a *close* second; but, as they say, close only counts in horseshoes and hand grenades. So great were the advantages of the firstborn in those days that when twins were born, a midwife would fix a red thread around the arm of the firstborn so they would not confused. Esau needed no red thread: his hair was red.

Jacob, however, had designs on Esau's inheritance. One day Jacob was at home, as usual, in the kitchen, as usual, cooking some pottage. Esau was, as usual, out in the fields. Esau came in starved and begged Jacob for some of his stew. Jacob gave Esau a bowl, but not until Esau had traded to Jacob, in return, his own birthright. Not until the bowl was empty and his stomach was full did Esau realize what he had done and what Jacob had done to him.

But Jacob and his mother were not through with their schemes. In Rebekah's eyes, Jacob deserved not only Esau's birthright, but also Isaac's blessing which was promised to Esau. So when she overheard Isaac say to Esau, "Go kill some game; make me a stew, and I will give you my blessing," her mind got to work. She coached Jacob in an act of deceit.

Jacob went into Isaac's room with a bowl of stew, dressed in Esau's clothes and wearing animal skins on his arms and neck so that he would feel and smell like Esau. The old and blind Isaac, fooled by Jacob's disguise, took the stew and gave to Jacob the blessing he thought he was giving to Esau.

Esau returned and discovered Jacob's treachery. He had once more been tripped up by Jacob, "the supplanter," and began to

Jacob

plot to kill him. But Rebekah discovered Esau's plans and sent Jacob far away to the house of her brother, Laban.

So, fleeing Esau's revenge, Jacob left home and headed to Haran. Who could imagine! The future father of the twelve tribes of Israel—a young man of doubtful character who had cheated his brother, deceived his father, and was dominated by his mother—was now running from the past, from trouble, and from home.

And what happened as he ran from home? He ran headlong into the Lord Almighty.

En route to Haran Jacob put his head on a stone, went to sleep, and began to dream. What you might expect would be a nightmarish dream, guilty and disturbed. God could have given him a lecture on honesty and family living, a hellfire, damnation sermon. Instead, God gave him a glimpse of heaven. In the dream heaven opened up and a ladder came down, spanning heaven and earth, with angels ascending and descending. It was sheer beauty and holiness. And instead of the "blessing out" he deserved, God gave him a message of blessed assurance: "Jacob, I am the God of Abraham and Isaac. I will give you this land upon which you stand. I will give it to you and your descendants who will be as numerous as the specks of dust on the earth." And if that were not enough, he added, "I will go with you and protect you" (see Gen. 28:13-15).

Isn't that just like our God? He doesn't give according to what we deserve but what we most need. When we most need it and least deserve it He comes to save, to comfort, and to bless us. For our God is a God of free grace. Do we deserve the Lord Christ? No more than Jacob deserved that dream. Deserving a blessing out, we get instead blessed assurance.

And we do as Jacob did. We mark those times and places where God comes as holy. Jacob took the stone he had used for a pillow, poured oil over it, and named the place *Bethel*—which means "the house of God." We each have our places where God has come to meet us. Those places are our Bethels.

But that was not all that Jacob did there, and what he did next is a mirror of us all. After having received free grace he turned it into a bargain, or tried.

He made a vow: "*If* you will give me bread to eat and clothes for my back, then I will go wherever you send me and I'll even give you a tithe" (see Gen. 28:20-22).

It was well meant, just as much of our bargaining with God is well meant: "Lord, if you just get me out of this mess, I'll change things, I'll be in church every Sunday, I'll be good; I'll even start tithing."

God came with a promise of sheer grace, no preconditions, no strings. Jacob couldn't believe it and turned it into a bargain. Oh, the vow was more than just a vow, more than bargaining. It was probably mixed with gratitude for the night before—just as our faith is a mixture of bargaining for grace and gratitude for grace. But unable to receive grace for what it is, full and free, Jacob tried to make a deal for it. So Jacob's journey is much like ours: trying to bargain for grace that cannot be bought but only given; freely given and freely received. We sing "Amazing Grace" and still try to earn God's love. I overheard one Sunday School teacher teaching her class of children new words to the song, "Jesus Loves Me": "Jesus loves me when I'm good." Of course He does, but also when we're bad: "For while we were still being sinners Christ died for us" (see Rom. 5:8).

Well, most vows get broken, and bargaining for grace is like trying to bottle the wind; so the next twenty years of Jacob's life were filled with one misadventure after another. And God, the God of Bethel's dream, seemed to move out of the picture altogether.

Jacob arrived at Laban's house and promptly fell in love with Rachel. When he got to Haran and saw that pretty young woman watering the flocks, it was love at first sight. So he bargained with his uncle to work for him seven years to marry Rachel. Scripture records that Jacob was so much in love that the years seemed like just a few days. Coleridge said of Jacob: "No man who could love like that could be wholly bad."

When the seven years were up Jacob spent his first blissful night with Rachel, only to discover the next morning that the woman next to him in bed was not Rachel, but Rachel's sister, Leah, who was not nearly as pretty and whom he certainly did not love.

Laban had pulled a fast one. He had outconned the con artist. Law required that he marry off his oldest daughter first. That was Leah. Laban had failed to mention that little detail seven years before, and Jacob failed to read the fine print.

You can imagine Jacob's consternation when he awoke and found out that Rachel was, in fact, Leah. In the Midrash, the Jewish commentary on the Old Testament, the rabbis have inserted this conversation into the story. When Jacob woke up and saw Leah next to him he complained to Leah:

"All night long I was calling you Rachel and you answered me; why did you deceive me?"

"And you," she retorted, "your father called you Esau and you answered; why did you deceive him?"[2] Ouch!

Greater love hath no man than to work fourteen years for a woman. When Jacob discovered that he was stuck with Leah, he bargained with his father-in-law that if he could have Rachel for his wife, as well, he would work for seven more years.

So now he had two wives—Leah and Rachel. The sisters began a contest to see who could accumulate the most babies; and eventually Jacob was the proud father of twelve sons. That is how we got the twelve tribes of Israel!

Twenty years after his arrival, Jacob left with his two wives, a caravan of children, and a large herd of livestock, all of which he had acquired with a combination of his wits and God's blessing. He was heading home.

And now he sat on the bank of the Jabbok River, looking back and looking ahead. Looking back was no picnic. He could not measure up to Grandfather Abraham or Father Isaac: dominated by his mother, passed over by his father, hated by his brother, manipulated by his father-in-law, and henpecked by both his wives. And he had treated them scarcely better. There was nothing in his life to feel good about but one small dream dreamed long ago.

The future looked no better. Esau was coming to meet him with four hundred men. When Jacob heard Esau was on his way, he sent a long trail of livestock to Esau, a belated peace offering—or guilt offering. Jacob was still bargaining, after all these years. Whether the gifts he sent would turn Esau's anger, he didn't know. There sat Jacob on the Jabbok riverbank in what you would call one dandy of a midcareer crisis.

Jacob had sent all the others across the stream ahead; now he was alone, wrestling with himself, filled with dread. But this night was to be a night of destiny—his life was about to be transfigured.

As Jacob waded out into the stream what happened is shrouded in the mystery of holiness. We see it "through a glass darkly"; we bow before it and take off our shoes lest we trample on holy ground.

What happened was a wrestling: fierce, decisive, agonized, and long, all night long. The narrative tells us that he whom Jacob wrestled was a "man." Later Scriptures called him an "angel." After the battle Jacob said it was God himself.

Fighting for his life, Jacob wrestled with the One with no name. Near dawn, just when Jacob thought he was winning, his opponent reached out, touched Jacob's hip, and wrenched it out of its socket.

The Other said, "Let me go, for dawn is breaking."

Jacob answered, "I will not let you go unless you bless me."

And the Opponent said, "What is your name?"

Jacob answered, "Jacob" (supplanter, cheat).

Whereupon the Other said, "Your name shall no longer be Jacob but Israel—for you have wrestled with God and have prevailed."

Jacob then asked, "What is your name?"

"Why do you wish to know?" the Other replied, then blessed him and left (see Gen. 32:26-29). Jacob limped to the other side of the river, wounded but transformed, dragging one leg but renamed Israel.

Jacob never got the name of the Other that night, but he knew

Whom he had hold of that night and Who had hold of him. He gave a name to the place of the struggle. "Peniel" he named it, because, in his words, "I have seen God face to face; yet I live." Peniel means "The face of God," and because he had seen God face to face and lived he knew the face to be that of grace.

But that was not all. Grace happened again the next day in the encounter between the two brothers. For as Jacob hobbled to Esau, bowing seven times in humility and repentance, Esau ran to meet him, grabbed him around the neck, and kissed him. And they wept tears of reunion joy.

The struggle by night and the embrace by day did not go unconnected by Jacob. Jacob said to Esau: "To see your face is like seeing the face of God" (33:10). Peniel had moved from wrestling at night with God to an embrace by day between brothers. And that story is ours as well. We, like Jacob, have met God, we who are deceptive, confused, and weak. We have survived not only Peniel, where we saw God's face, but Golgotha, too, where we killed His Son. And we have survived not only to live but also to be grasped by an incalculable love. We have experienced the living God whose name and face is love. And we have experienced that same love in the face of Esau as well, the church by miracle of God's grace having become God's face to us.

So Jacob, now Israel, limped into a future toward a grace he could not earn, but could only be given, striving with God and man till all bargaining ceases and there is only grace. His journey is ours. Glimpses of heaven cannot completely break earth's pull; there is still some Jacob left in Israel (and in us). But we have met the One whose name is grace, and we will never be the same.

Charles Wesley's great hymn has joined Jacob's story and the gospel story:

> Come, O thou Traveller unknown,
> Whom still I hold but cannot see!
> My company before is gone,
> And I am left alone with thee;
> With thee all night I mean to stay,
> And wrestle till the break of day.

> My prayer hath power with God; the grace
>   Unspeakable I now receive;
> Through faith I see thee face to face,
>   I see thee face to face and live!
> In vain I have not wept and strove;
>   Thy nature and thy name is Love.

Near the end of his life Jacob said this blessing. I now say it to you in benediction. "May God in whose presence my fathers Abraham and Isaac walked, may God who has been my shepherd from my birth unto this day, may the angel who has been my savior from all harm, bless these boys" (Gen. 48:15-16, *The Jerusalem Bible*). And bless you. Amen.

Notes

1. Clarence Edward Macartney, *Sermons on Old Testament Heroes* (Nashville: Abingdon Press, 1935), p. 100.
2. Elie Wiesel, *Messengers of God: Biblical Portraits and Legends* (New York: Random House, 1976), p. 115.

4
Joseph

Joseph: There is no story in the Bible more carefully crafted, no story filled as full with the range of human passions as this one. In it you find political intrigue and sibling rivalry, love and hate, jealousy and compassion, lust and ambition, heroism and pity. Joseph is the hero; but the major actor is God Himself, not directly but in the midst of the story's wild mixture of human passions. Through the turns and twists of its plot we see the glimmer of a truth that somewhere behind it all there is a God who knows us and who cares, a God who makes out of all of our stories one story and from all our crazy goings-on one plot. Joseph points to this truth at the end of the story. His brothers were cowering before him, fearful that now with their father, Jacob, dead, Joseph would take revenge on them for selling him into slavery. And what does Joseph say?

"Do not be afraid. Who am I to be in God's place? *No, you meant it for evil but God meant it for good*" (see Gen. 50:19-20).

It was a brave statement of faith in the power and purpose of God. It was brave because it was said looking at evil face to face. Joseph had not passed lightly over evil. He had passed through it.

The story begins as Joseph turns seventeen. He was the apple of his father's eye and Jacob's favorite. How ironic! Jacob himself was passed over: his own father, Isaac, preferred Esau to him. Jacob knew the pain of seeing his father favor his brother Esau, yet he played favorites with his son Joseph. How much like us—despite our protests and promises to the contrary, we repeat the mistakes of our parents. It all speaks, I suppose, to the stubborn tenaciousness of original sin.

Joseph was the favored son of his father; he knew it, he loved it, and he flaunted it. Jacob gave him a coat of many colors and Joseph wore it like a neon sign that read: "Father loves me best." Spoiled, he craved attention; a dandy, he fancied the way he looked.

His brothers hated him, and we can understand that. The story says that they would not even speak peaceably to him—they would not even extend the daily shalom. Or (as James Sanders translates it into our vernacular), they wouldn't even give him the time of day.

One day Joseph went to his brothers and said: "Listen to my latest dream. We were gathering wheat in the field when suddenly my bundle stood up and all of yours formed a circle around mine and bowed down to it." His brothers didn't have to be Sigmund Freud to get the point. "What!" they answered angrily, "You wish to reign over us?!"

Undaunted, Joseph told them a second dream—this one even more preposterous: "I saw the sun, the moon, and eleven stars prostrate before me." That was too much even for his doting father, Jacob. "What!" said Jacob, "Are you so like God your parents and brothers are to bow down to you?" (see Gen. 37:1-10).

Because of the dreams his brothers hated him even more. They began a plot to kill him. One day Jacob sent Joseph to Shechem to meet his brothers. Did Jacob not see how his favoritism had caused them to hate Joseph? Why did he not foresee the danger? Later the mixture of grief and guilt over questions like these would nearly kill him.

When Joseph met his brothers they jumped him. They tore off his coat of many colors and threw him into a pit. While they were debating over how to dispose of him, Judah saw a passing caravan and talked his brothers into selling him into slavery.

They meant it for evil, but God meant it for good.

According to the Genesis text, Joseph was silent all during the brutal attack. No pleading, no bargaining. Silence.

Joseph

Why the silence? The Jewish imagination of Elie Wiesel asks: Did it cross Joseph's mind that his father might be behind all this? Had not Jacob sent him there?[1]

Did the story of Mount Moriah sweep over Joseph—the story of Abraham's sacrifice of Isaac? Was his father, Jacob, given as he was to feelings of inferiority, trying to match the heroic faith of Abraham? Was he offering his *own* favorite son? Why else would Jacob have sent him there? The *terror* Joseph must have felt, not just at the violence of his brothers but of the thought that Jacob might be behind it all!

The two episodes, Moriah and Shechem, both speak to the providence of God. Both began in terror and ended in a miracle: Isaac was saved by the sudden appearance of a ram, Joseph by a passing caravan. Joseph was saved! But the questions had to persist. And does the memory of Moriah and Shechem spark our own Christian imaginations—to another son led to slaughter, like a lamb mute before his shearers, this one not saved as the other two, but raised from the dead to be the Saving One?

The brothers, meanwhile, returned with a lie for their father. They dipped Joseph's coat of many colors into a goat's blood and took it to Jacob. Jacob jumped to the conclusion that the brothers intended: "a wild beast has killed my son!" O cruel irony. Jacob, who as a young man dressed up like Esau and deceived his father Isaac, was now deceived by his own sons. The guilt and grief nearly killed him. He cried out, "I will wear my mourning clothes until I die." And he nearly did.

Joseph in the meantime was brought down to Egypt a slave. The Scriptures say, "And the Lord was with Joseph" (39:2), just as the Lord is always with the oppressed and downtrodden. God is always on the side of the slaves; the Lord is with them.

From his beginnings as a slave, however, Joseph achieved stunning success—first as an interpreter of dreams, second as a statesman, the king's right-hand man.

Joseph, like a cat, landed on his feet. He succeeded in whatever tasks he had. First of all, he became Potiphar's trusted servant, the manager of his house. As an extraordinarily handsome young man, he also attracted women. The plot thickens.

The Talmud has a story about Joseph in Potiphar's house: One day a group of high society ladies came to Potiphar's house for lunch. Madame Potiphar served citrus fruits and gave each lady a knife to peel them with. In walked Joseph. So moved and bedazzled were the ladies that they went into a state of shock and all of them cut their hands with the knives. Madame Potiphar breathlessly moaned: "This is what I must endure day after day, hour after hour."[2]

You see, Joseph had turned the head of Potiphar's wife. The next verses in the Bible read like a soap opera. Potiphar's wife fell deeply in love with her young servant. She made many overtures to him. Repeatedly, however, he refused her advances. (That part is quite *unlike* the soap operas.)

Then one day when the house was empty save for the two of them, Madame Potiphar cornered him and moved aggressively to win him. He ran away in a panic, leaving his coat in her hands.

Joseph had the choice: sin or trouble. He refused to sin; his next step was jail. The jilted Madame Potiphar took revenge by accusing Joseph of her own sins (a familiar human foible). "Hell hath no fury like a woman scorned," the saying goes; and Joseph found himself in jail, falsely accused of seducing his boss's wife.

She meant it for evil, but God meant it for good.

Joseph was in jail. The text again says, "And the Lord was with Joseph" (39:21). And, again, Joseph made the best of a bad situation. He made friends with the jailers. Soon he was the administrative director of the jail. Have you known people like that? Joseph, like a cat, had again landed on his feet.

He became the king's private psychoanalyst and interpreted the famous dream of the seven fat cows and seven skinny ones. "There will be seven bountiful years of harvest," said Joseph, "and seven years of famine." "You had better get prepared," said Joseph. "You've got a job," said Pharaoh. The Pharaoh was so impressed that he made Joseph his right-hand man, prince, and chief bureaucrat, with one difference from ours—Joseph's plans worked! Because of Joseph's shrewd administration Egypt was prepared and not only survived the famine but also became during that time the caretaker of nations around it. By God's will this nation of industry and plenty looked after the starving nations around its borders. Not a bad biblical precedent. That is the way the biblical God uses the nations He blesses; that is the way He blesses through the nations He uses.

During those years Joseph became a powerful prince, married an Egyptian princess, and had two sons: *Manasseh,* which means "For God has made me forget all my tribulation," and *Ephraim,* which means "For God has made me bear fruit in the land of my misery."

The predicted famine brought an unexpected turn in the story. Joseph's ten brothers—minus Benjamin—came to Joseph's court seeking grain.

Had Joseph forgotten, had he forgiven them? When they came and bowed before him the Scriptures record that he "remembered the dreams which he had dreamed of them" (42:9). You remember —their stalks of wheat bowing down to his stalk. We get no glimpse of *how* he remembered the dream—whether he chuckled to himself with gleeful revenge or whether his memory was choked with pity. But we do know that with the passing of the days ahead Joseph won victory over bitterness.

Joseph did not then tell them who he was, but he set to work trying to reunite the family. He maneuvered a way to get his brothers to bring back his brother Benjamin and then their father Jacob. On the first trip back they brought Benjamin. Then as they set about to leave, Joseph planted a silver cup in Benjamin's saddlebags. He sent his soldiers to confiscate the cup and bring his brothers back. When they were brought before him, Joseph gave the verdict: Benjamin had to stay and become his slave.

Brother Judah came before Joseph and pleaded that he might take Benjamin's place. He told Joseph (whom he still did not recognize) that his father Jacob had nearly died over the death of his son Joseph and that if Benjamin were taken away, that would finish him for good. Judah cried out: "I cannot bear to see this disaster come upon my father."

With this show of love, Joseph could not hold back his identity any longer. He broke down and cried and told them who he was— their brother Joseph, whom they had sold into slavery.

You can imagine that the first response of the brothers was fear. Wouldn't Joseph go ahead and wreak revenge? Instead, Joseph conquered vengefulness and bitterness and forgave them. He called for a family reunion and had Jacob brought to Egypt.

His response to their fear was remarkable. His vision was not tribal or national but global. It embraced the overarching providence of God. "Do not grieve that you sold me into slavery. God sent me here to save the lives of many. What's more, he sent me here to save *your* lives. So it was not you who sent me here. God did. And he made me a ruler here. So, never you mind, go get Father Jacob and bring him here." And they did.

His brothers would be afraid once more—when Jacob died. Joseph had promised Jacob that he would forgive his brothers and do them no harm. But now Jacob was dead. Would Joseph keep the promise?

The brothers came to Joseph and, trembling with fear, said, "Please forgive us the evil that we did to you." When Joseph heard them he wept and said:

"Do not be afraid. For am I in God's place?" You can imagine the twinkle in his eye. That is exactly how he saw himself when he was a boy and dreamed the dream of the sun and moon and eleven stars bowing down to him. But now as one remarkably wise, mellowed by years and God, he said:

"Do not be afraid. For am I in God's place? You meant evil against me but God meant it for good."

You meant it for evil, but God meant it for good.

That is a vision from eternal places. That is an affirmation of faith in the power and purpose of a good God.

Can you believe God can take evil and turn it to good? Can you believe He can take the evil done to *you* and turn it into good? Can you believe that God can turn the evil *you* have done into good?

Can you believe that He can take the evil of our selling our brother into slavery and make it our salvation?[3]

This belief is no simplistic notion that the evil we see in the world is not evil but good! It is the stubborn faith that there is no evil dark enough that God somehow, someway, sometime cannot redeem, that no matter how dark it is, the darkness will not overcome the light. It is the stubborn faith Paul expressed in Romans 8:28: "We know that in everything God works for good with those who love him."

What kind of God is this who allows suffering only, then, to use it for good? What kind of God is it who can take evil done us and turn it into good? What kind of God is it who can take *our* evil and use it for *our* salvation?

It's the kind of God who was with Joseph in slavery and in jail; the kind of God who was with a baby in the bullrushes and who used that baby, Moses, to free some Jews from Pharaoh's grip; the kind of God who was in a Hebrew baby's crib in a cow stall outside Bethlehem; the kind of God who hung on a gallows outside Jerusalem; the kind of God who held back not even His own Son.

What kind of God is it who can take our crucifying of His only one-of-a-kind Son and turn it into our salvation?

It's the God of Abraham and Isaac and Jacob and Joseph and Jesus, that's who.

We say it bravely. We say it sometimes with tears. We say it sometimes with hardly any breath at all because the breath has been knocked out of us. We say it sometimes without seeing it, without feeling it, for "we walk by faith, not sight" (2 Cor. 5:7).

But we say it: They meant it for evil; you meant it for evil; we meant it for evil; but God means it for good.

Notes

1. Elie Wiesel, *Messengers of God* (New York: Random House, 1976), p. 165 ff.
2. Ibid., p. 148.
3. This turn of questions was suggested to me by James S. Sanders, *God Has a Story Too* (Philadelphia: Fortress Press, 1979), p. 53 ff.

5
Moses

Moses—"Everytime Hollywood cranks out a movie about him, Buechner says, "they always give the part to somebody like Charlton Heston with some fake whiskers glued on."[1] Actually Heston is not too bad a choice. Scripture says that Moses was an uncommonly handsome child. No doubt he was a striking figure of a man. Is there a more heroic figure in all of art than Michelangelo's statue of Moses? But as striking as his looks were, these could not compare with the magnitude of his place in history.

Moses—the most powerful hero in the Bible. Moses—the man who changed the course of history. Moses—the man who brought us the Law of God. Moses—whose grave was hidden by God so that it would not be worshiped. Moses—a man so great that, according to Jude 9, when he died the archangel Michael and the devil fought over his body. Moses—"the man over whose body heaven and hell fought."[2]

There is no more poignant picture in the Bible than the last days of Moses.

After forty years of wandering in the wilderness, Moses had finally led the Jews to the border of Canaan, the Promised Land. Now God led him to the top of Mount Pisgah, and from the peak of that mountain God showed him the Promised Land. And Moses could see glimpses of it all: the River Jordan, the Sea of Galilee, the Dead Sea, Jerusalem, even the glint of the great Mediterranean Sea. It took his breath. His heart leaped.

But then came the words of God that broke his heart: "Moses, this is the land I promised Abraham and Isaac and Jacob. I now have let you see it, but I will not let you enter it" (see Deut. 34:4). From breathtaking joy to heartbreaking sorrow. He could see it, but he could not lead the people in. For reasons difficult for us to understand, his people now would go on without him.

One hundred twenty years old, standing on Mount Pisgah with a lump in his throat too big to swallow, fighting back the tears, Moses thought back, as far as he could remember, over his long, remarkable, and turbulent life.

Actually his life began before Moses knew that it began. It began in the heart of God. Before he knew God, God knew him. Before he picked God, God had picked him out and planned to use him to accomplish His purpose: to free His people from Pharaoh and to found a faith based on the law of God, a covenant faith.

God prepared the way for Moses before Moses left his mother's womb. The paranoid Pharaoh, fearful of the growing ranks of Jews, ordered the midwives in Egypt to strangle all the Jewish baby boys at birth. But as Scripture says: "The midwives feared God and did not do as the king of Egypt commanded" (Ex. 1:17). What a remarkable incident. *The fear of God in the heart of a nurse is mightier than the pharaohs of this world.* Or, as Paul said, "God hath chosen the weak things of the world to confound the things which are mighty" (1 Cor. 1:27, KJV).

But, determined still, the Pharaoh ordered all Jewish baby boys thrown into the Nile. This is where Moses comes in.

Moses' beginnings.—When Moses was born, his mother hid him in a basket which was placed among the bullrushes in the Nile. The pharaoh's daughter just happened to be bathing in the Nile River nearby and discovered the basket and the baby. She named him Moses because the name means "to be taken from the water."

Who would have believed that she just happened to be bathing at that part of the Nile that day, and just happened to see the basket, and just happened to find as a nurse for the baby Moses' own mother? Some might call that coincidence. People of faith choose to call it providence.

Out of the wondrous working of God's purpose, this fine, handsome Jewish boy charmed everyone he met and found himself raised in the Pharaoh's house and given the best education Egypt and the ancient world had to offer.

However, his being raised among the privileged ruling class of Egypt did not cause him to reject his own people. He could have, of course, lived a life of leisure. Instead, as Scripture records: "He grew up and went out to see his own people" (see 2:11). And when he saw them his heart went out to them in their suffering and slavery. So touched was he that he risked everything to intervene. It was a drama to be repeated hundreds and thousands of times—the divine sympathy moving men and women to act—Saint Francis, Sojourner Truth, Dietrich Bonhoeffer, Martin Luther King.

The Midrash tells us that Moses first tried to work within the system to make life for his people more tolerable.[3] Then, as the Bible records, one day he saw an Egyptian overseer torturing a Jewish slave. He looked around, saw no witnesses, then threw himself upon the Egyptian and killed him.

The next day he saw two Jews quarreling and tried to break up the fight. "Why do you strike your brother?" Moses asked. The man answered insolently: "Who made you prince and judge over us?" And then the clincher: "Are you planning to kill us too?" (see 2:13-14). Somehow the man knew Moses' secret: that he had killed an Egyptian to save a Jew and that he himself was Jewish.

Denounced, betrayed, and afraid of the Pharaoh's sword, Moses fled from Egypt to Midian. There he married a priest's daughter, raised a family, and lived a peaceful life for forty years.

Did he forget the plight of his people? For forty years he made no attempt to go back, settled down with his adopted family, and, for all appearances, seems to have forgotten them.

Why? Elie Wiesel, the master Jewish storyteller, has one plausible explanation: it was because he was so disillusioned with his own people. While he was in Egypt they made no attempt to resist and rebel; they had settled into a kind of resigned acceptance of their slavery. Then they seemed so petty, so given to infighting. But perhaps the cruelest blow of all: there was only one person who could have been the informer who told on Moses—that he had killed the Egyptian—and that person was the very Jew he had saved! Was all this not reason enough why Moses had fled and stayed away, why Midian would become the land of forgetting? It was not Pharaoh. In Wiesel's words: "His fear of Pharaoh was insignificant compared to his disillusionment with the Jews!"[4]

But as Yahweh went down with Joseph into Egypt, so He also went with Moses from Egypt to Midian.

The call of Moses.—Moses was tending his flock one day when he saw a burning bush. Wondering why it kept on burning, he went over to investigate. A voice said "Moses." "Here am I." "Come no nearer," said the voice; "take off your shoes. This is holy ground."

The voice then said: "I have seen the miserable condition of my people in Egypt. I have heard their cry. Now I intend to deliver them out of slavery. And, Moses, I send you to Pharaoh, to bring the children of Israel, my people, out of slavery" (see 3:1-12).

Once and for all God declared Himself on the side of the oppressed. God is not neutral on the issue of freedom. His heart goes out to those who are enslaved. God is not a detached observer when it comes to justice. God sides with the poor and the weak. The question is not whose side God is on. The Bible is unmistakably clear on that. The question is: Whose side are *we* on?

When God called Moses, Moses argued all he could. Why me? Why not an angel? Why not my older brother Aaron? I stutter. I'm married, have a family. I have responsibilities to my father-in-law. And what am I supposed to tell the Jews when they start asking questions? What shall I say? And what will I tell Pharaoh? And who shall I say sent me? Why me? Question upon question. The Midrash says it took seven days for God to persuade Moses to go.

But persuade him God did. There is a charming story from the Jewish Midrash about how God chose and persuaded Moses. While Moses was tending the sheep of his father-in-law in Midian, one young kid ran away from the flock. Moses searched for it until it reached a ravine where it found a well from which to drink. When Moses reached the young kid he said, "I did not know that you were thirsty. Now you must be weary." And he carried the kid back to the flock. Then God said, "Because thou hast shown pity in leading back one of a flock belonging to a man, thou shalt lead my flock, Israel."[5] It is God who calls and God who qualifies. Yes, Moses was a murderer; but now he was God's chosen servant. Yes, he stammered; but as Martin Buber said, "It is laid upon the stammering to bring the voice of Heaven to Earth."[6]

Then God gave His name to Moses. Before this moment no one had ever known God's name. "Yahweh," we say it in Hebrew: I am who I am, I cause to be what I cause to be. But the Jews still will not pronounce it even though they know it, so deep is their reverence. They stutter when they say God's name. Would that we were so reverent. We throw God's name around so carelessly. Jews won't pronounce God's name. We put it on bumper stickers.

And God gave Moses new powers, all the powers he would need—God always empowers us to do what He calls us to do—and God gave Moses his brother Aaron to make his speeches for him.

Exodus records what happened next in feverish pace: Moses pleading with Pharaoh, Aaron having to *convince* the Jews to leave Egypt—how frightening freedom sometimes is and how comfortable slavery seems.

Pharaoh's heart was hard, and God had to send ten plagues, only the last one breaking through its hardness. You can feel in your bones the darkness and light, the terror and excitement of that last night in Egypt. The firstborn child of every Egyptian family dying, the angel of death passing over only the Jewish homes. Pharaoh, grieving the death of his own son, finally saying yes. You can hear the mournful sobs of parents, Moses' lieutenants jostling and exhorting the people, "Let's go, fast, faster before Pharaoh changes his mind."

The people left Egypt and then found themselves boxed in, the Red Sea just ahead, Pharaoh's troops right behind. Pharaoh *had* changed his mind.

The people panicked but Moses said, "Stop your crying; the Lord will save you." Then he stretched out his hand. A strong easterly wind blew back the waters, and the people crossed the sea. Then as Pharaoh's horses and chariots followed, the waters swept back again and the Egyptians were drowned.

The Jews had been saved. And Moses, the stutterer, let loose with one of the most beautiful songs of Scripture: "He has covered himself in glory,/horse and rider he has thrown into the sea./ Yahweh is my strength, my song,/he is my salvation" (15:1-2, *The Jerusalem Bible*).

The people crossed the desert to Mount Sinai where God brought the greatest moment of all: He revealed His Word, His

Law. The history of faith now reaches a new dimension. "I bore you on eagles' wings and brought you to myself," He said to Moses. "... If you will obey my voice ... you shall be my own possession among all peoples; for all the earth is mine" (Ex. 19:4-5).

On Sinai Moses heard God saying, "I have freed you from slavery. Now I show you how to *stay* free: by following My Law." Then amid thunder and lightning came the Ten Commandments:

"Thou shalt have no other gods before me.
Thou shalt not make unto thee any graven image.
Thou shalt not take the name of the Lord thy God in vain.
Remember the sabbath day, to keep it holy.
Honour thy father and thy mother.
Thou shalt not kill.
Thou shalt not commit adultery.
Thou shalt not steal.
Thou shalt not bear false witness against thy neighbor.
Thou shalt not covet" (20:3-17; KJV).

Moses stayed on that mountain for forty days, and when he came down the mountain he couldn't believe his eyes and ears.

The people were dancing and singing round a golden calf like a bunch of pagans. And who was leading them but Moses' own brother Aaron, head of the worship committee. Nobody knows, comments Buechner, whether this was Aaron's way of getting even with his kid brother Moses for all those years of playing second fiddle or "whether he actually believed with the rest of mankind that a God in the hand is worth two in the bush."[7]

Well, whatever the reasons, Moses was so angry when he saw what was going on that he threw down the tablets containing the Commandments and broke them into a hundred pieces.

He had had just about enough. This was close to the last straw. What was he to do with this stiff-necked, faithless, belly-aching people?

No sooner had they left Egypt than they were already complaining: Why did you make us leave? Did you lead us out of Egypt so that we would die in the desert?

Three days after the miraculous crossing of the Red Sea, they were complaining about something to drink. And a month later they were complaining about something to eat: "Let's go back to

Egypt—at least there we had plenty to eat!" Even after God sent them manna to eat they bellyached. At one point Moses cried out, "O God, what am I to do with this ungrateful people? One more incident and they will stone me to death!"

On another occasion he had to remind them that he had taken nothing from them and that he had not gotten rich at their expense. One only says that when he has been accused.

"Who knows," suggests Wiesel, "Perhaps God's decision not to let him enter the promised land was meant as a reward rather than as punishment."[8]

And yet as troublesome and disappointing as they were, Moses would not forsake them. He even defended them against God's anger.

When God saw His people dancing around the golden calf, He was so angry that He wanted to destroy them and told Moses so. But Moses pleaded with God, saying that God should not free His people only to turn around and kill them; and to make his point further he reminded God of His promise to Abraham and Isaac and Jacob.

Then Moses' heart broke and he said to God: "If you refuse to forgive them and destroy them, then go ahead and wipe my name out of your Book of Life too!"

Moses became as one parent defending a child to the other parent. God said to Moses: "Your people have sinned." And we can almost hear Moses saying: "When they are good they are yours, but when they are bad are they mine?"[9]

Moses pleaded and prayed, and God Almighty heard the prayer of this Jew and changed His mind! He did not destroy them!

We get the picture of this great hero trying to pull God to His people and trying to pull His people to God. Moses: trying to pull heaven and earth together with his bare hands. What an amazement: that Moses would stay faithful to such a people! What an amazement: that God would forgive and save us!

How did Moses keep on? Occasionally, just to keep him going, Moses would ask God for some sign, some assurance that he was still doing what God wanted.

And God obliged. Remember that day when God showed Moses His glory? God swept by, hiding Moses in a cleft of a rock, sheltering him with his hand. It was a new experience of God. "I will make all my goodness pass before you," said God. It was the experience on which is based the John 3:16 of the Old Testament, Exodus 34:6: "The Lord God is merciful and gracious, slow to anger, and abounding in steadfast love and faithfulness." Grace. It was for but a moment; and although all Moses saw was His back, it was enough to keep him going for the rest of his life, until that day when God showed him the Promised Land from Mount Pisgah and then called him home.

When Moses heard the word from God about his death, he spent his last hours blessing the tribes of Israel, all twelve. Then he began his climb up Mount Nebo. Slowly he entered the cloud waiting for him. Looking back, he could no longer see his people. Tears welled up.

Jewish tradition describes his death this way:

> When he reached the top of the mountain, he halted. You have one more minute, God warned him, so as not to deprive him of his right to death. And Moses lay down. And God said: Close your eyes. And Moses closed his eyes. And God said: Fold your arms across your chest. And Moses folded his arms across his chest. Then, silently, God kissed his lips. And the soul of Moses found shelter in God's breath and was swept away into eternity.[10]

As Scripture says, "So Moses died . . . by the mouth of Yahweh" (see Deut. 34:5).

And at the foot of the mountain the Jews wept for thirty days, partly out of guilt for how they had treated him, partly out of grief for the loss of their leader and the part of God he brought to them. They grieved the death of this man, this lonely, passionate, and powerful prophet of God.

And from that time, deep within their hearts was born a hope, a hope that defied all circumstances: a hope that another would come, a new Moses, but greater than the first—with a new law, this one not written on stone but in our hearts, this one not based on our frail wills but upon the grace of God.

And come he did, the new Moses, with a New Covenant, not to abolish Moses and the Prophets but to fulfill them.

Notes

1. Frederick Buechner, *Peculiar Treasures* (New York: Harper & Row, 1979), p. 110.
2. Clarence E. Macartney, *Sermons On Old Testament Heroes* (Nashville: Abingdon Press, 1935), p. 183.
3. Elie Wiesel, *Messengers of God* (New York: Random House, 1976), p. 185.
4. Ibid., pp. 188-9.
5. C. G. Montefiore, H. Loewe, eds., *A Rabbinic Anthology* (London: Macmillan, 1938), p. 45.
6. Martin Buber, *Moses: The Revelation and the Covenant* (New York: Harper & Row Torchbook, 1958), p. 59.
7. Buechner, p. 2.
8. Wiesel, p. 199.
9. From Midrash found in Montefiore, p. 243.
10. The prose version of Elie Wiesel, p. 204.

6
Elijah, 1

Elijah, part 1, is the story of a man so great that Jewish tradition places him side by side, shoulder to shoulder, with Moses. Moses, the Lawgiver; Elijah, Prophet of prophets. Moses and Elijah represent the Law and the Prophets. To this day in the Jewish Passover meal, a cup of wine is placed on the table and left undrunk in honor of Elijah and in expectation of his return.

Elijah—A man so great that when Jesus walked on earth some Jews exclaimed, "Look, it is Elijah." Elijah—the man whom God chose, along with Moses, to meet Christ face to face on the Mount of transfiguration, where they talked together concerning the cross. What made him so great, this man whose life is recorded in eight scant chapters in the Books of the Kings? Come along, hear his story, and find out.

We are abruptly introduced to Elijah in the seventeenth chapter of 1 Kings: "And Elijah the Tishbite, who was of the inhabitants of Gilead, said unto Ahab, As the Lord God of Israel liveth, before whom I stand, there shall not be dew nor rain these years, but according to my word" (17:1, KJV).

We catch him in midcareer, with no background information at all. But never mind, backgrounds do not make prophets; God does. Parents do not produce prophets; prophets are born of the Word of God. Prophets are men and women who hear God's Word and believe it, who see through the appearances of things in the world and see the world as it really is, who speak with courage what God's Spirit is saying. Prophets stand with a Bible in one hand and the morning newspaper in the other; they are keenly attuned to the Spirit of God on the one hand and to the signs of the times on the other—sensitive, to use Davie Napier's phrase, to "Word of God" and "Word of Earth."[1] Prophets are not so much *foretellers* as *forthtellers*. They *speak forth* God's word. The foresight they have comes from their keen insight into the Word of God and the word of earth.

Elijah was a forthteller. The Lord was the one before whom he stood, whom he served, and whose word he spoke.

To whom did Elijah speak forth this word? King Ahab. Poor Ahab had not one but two headaches. Headache number 1 was Elijah. In Buechner's words: "If, generally speaking, a prophet to a king was like ants to a picnic, Elijah was like a swarm of bees."[2] Ahab could not escape him. Headache number 2 was his wife Jezebel, a woman so evil she made Adolf Hitler look like Mr. Rogers. She was foreign-born and tried to shove her religion down the throats of the Jews. Baal worship was her religion, so idols and temples to Baal were set up all over the country. Under Jezebel's prompting the prophets of Yahweh were systematically killed. Now, Baal was not just Jezebel's religion; it was also the native religion of the country. So it didn't take much pushing for the people to swallow. To them it was the "old-time religion."

What was Baal religion? To this land of farmers it was the religion of fertility, the worship of nature with its cycles and seasons, the full harvest, the house full of children, the life of security. Its god was a god of rain, its Bible the *Farmer's Almanac*.

We don't have to look far to see that Baal worship is the native religion of our soil, too. Baalism is the religion of success, self, and sensuality. The religion of success: if it works, do it. The religion of self: if it serves me, do it. The religion of sensuality: if it feels good, do it.

Baalism knows no right and wrong; it has no ethic. Whatever gets results is OK. Whatever advances me is OK. Whatever feels good is OK. Baal is a god named Wall Street, a god named Madison Avenue, a god named Hollywood. It is the religion of the bottom line, the religion of "Watching Out for Number 1," the religion of "Go with the Flow."

"Wait!" you say, "Success is not sin. Selfhood is no sin. Sensuality is no sin. Lay no Puritan trip on me!" So let me explain. Success, selfhood, and sensuality are good gifts of God, just as the rain and harvest are gifts from God. But most evil is a distortion of the good; and when success, self, and sensuality become the meaning and end of life they become idols. When they change from gifts in life to the center of life's concern, then they become Baal.

Baalism is the religion of success, self, and sensuality. It is the pagan religion of every nation, tribe, and clan. And Yahweh God fights Baal in every generation.

Through the conniving of Jezebel and the compliance of her weak-kneed husband, Ahab, Baalism had once again become the dominant religion of Israel. Darkness covered the land as the light of God's Word grew dim, a candle flickering, about to go out.

Then crisis hit in the form of drought and famine. Elijah announced its coming to Ahab. Remember what he said: "Neither dew nor rain . . . except by my word" (17:1). As you could guess, this message did not endear Elijah to Ahab.

What they had was not only an economic crisis—no rain, no crops, no food—but also a religious crisis. What happens when Baal, the harvest god, stops producing? What happens when you worship success and success lets you down?

During the long drought Elijah was sustained by two unlikely sources. First of all, Elijah followed God's instructions and went to a brook named Cherith. There he drank its water and was fed by ravens.

Some modern scholars have tried to make this miracle more plausible to our "modern" minds with comical results. By changing a couple of vowels the Hebrew word could read instead of ravens *Arabs,* or, the same Hebrew word can mean *merchants.* Or, another proposal: since the root word for *ravens* means "to be black," why not assume that Elijah was fed by *blacks?* Imagine blacks or merchants or Arabs tramping through the wilderness to share their fried chicken with Elijah! I agree with Davie Napier: "Blacks feeding a white? Arabs feeding a Jew? Merchants feeding a prophet? Ravens is better."[3]

When the brook dried up, Elijah, again following God's instructions, moved far north and was sustained by a poor widow. She shared with him her meager rations, and miraculously her jars of meal and oil never ran empty no matter how much they ate.

Then, after a while, the widow's son took sick and was at the point of death. The widow said to Elijah: "Why did you come, you man of God: to expose my sin and kill my son!" (see 17:18). Crying out in grief she did what we all do: she went through a time of blaming God and blaming herself.

"Give me your son" (17:19), Elijah said; then, taking the book in an upper room, he prayed a prayer of protest. In the Bible we have not only prayers of thanksgiving, confession, and intercession but also prayers of protest.

Moses: "Why do you treat your servant so badly?" (Num. 11:11, *The Jerusalem Bible*).

Jeremiah: "Yahweh, you have deceived me" (see Jer. 20:7).

Habakkuk: "How long, Yahweh, am I to cry for help while you will not listen?" (Hab. 1:2, *The Jerusalem Bible*).

Elijah prayed: "Yahweh, My God, can it be your will to inflict this catastrophe on the very widow who has opened her home to me?" (see v. 21).

God heard the prayer. Elijah then took the child down to the mother and said, "See, your son lives" (v. 23). And so he did.

The drought continued for three and one-half years. After that long period of time, the Word of Yahweh came to Elijah: "You can go now to face Ahab. I am ready to let it rain over the land" (18:1). So Elijah went to confront Ahab.

When the two met, Ahab said: "Is it you, you troubler of Israel?" (18:17). And Elijah responded: "I'm not the one who troubles Isra-

Elijah, 1

el, but you and your kin, you are the troublers of Israel!" (see v. 18).

That same dialogue echoes through history between kings and prophets, between the world and the Word.

Martin Luther King was called a troubler of America. But he replied as Elijah did: "It is not I who trouble America, but you and your kin who build black and white drinking fountains, who deny to blacks equal education, who deny us a seat at Woolworth's and who show us to the back of the bus." King wasn't the troubler. He exposed the demon of racism in our land, and as he exorcised it in the name of Christ it rushed out with violence. The violence inherent in our land came painfully to the surface.

"You troubler of Israel," Ahab said. "No," replied Elijah, "you are the troubler."

The stage is now set for the dramatic showdown between Elijah and Ahab and between the prophets of Baal and the lone prophet of Yahweh. Elijah challenged the prophets of Baal to meet him on Mount Carmel.

Here is the scene. Two altars were erected on Mount Carmel, one to Baal, the other to Yahweh.

There were two altars; but there is only one true God, so Elijah lifted his voice with a challenge. A choice must be made. It's *either/or,* not *both/and.* You cannot worship both Baal *and* Yahweh. You must choose. "If [Yahweh] is God, follow him; but if Baal, then follow Him" (18:21).

The crowd grew quiet. They had tried, as we all do, to ignore the truth. They weren't rejecting Yahweh outright; they were just adding Baal—just for extra insurance. It's nice to have Yahweh God, delivering-from-Egypt God, history-making God, Law-giving God, and, just for security, to have Baal-god too: rain-making god, fertility-god, crop-insurance god.

They didn't want to say no to Yahweh. They wanted them both: Yahweh *and* Baal. They wanted it both ways.

But you cannot have it both ways. You cannot worship Yahweh

and success, Yahweh and self, Yahweh and sensuality. You can't have your Yahweh and Baal-god, too.

This is how Elijah put it to the people: "How long will you go limping with two different opinions?" (RSV). "How long do you mean to hobble first on one leg and then on the other?" (*The Jerusalem Bible*). "How long will you sit on the fence?" (NEB).

How long can you live divided up inside? How long can you live in double-mindedness? Here is great truth, psychologically, spiritually, and ethically. You cannot keep straddling the fence. Choose we must. "Know yourself," said Socrates. Kierkegaard said it better: "Choose yourself." The self we are is determined by whom we follow. Not to choose is to live a divided self. "No one can serve two masters," Jesus said, "[You'll] hate the one and love the other, [you'll] be devoted to one and despise the other. You can't serve God and mammon" (Matt. 6:24), both God and money, both Yahweh and Baal.

How long will you go limping in two directions at once? Choose this day whom you will serve. If Yahweh is God, follow him; if Baal is God, follow him!

With the crowd sitting in uneasy silence, Elijah laid down the terms of the contest. "Bring two bulls. You prepare one on your altar," he said to the prophets of Baal, "and I'll prepare one on my altar. You pray to your God and I'll pray to mine. The God who answers by sending fire, *He* is God" (see vv. 23-24).

The people responded with a shout. The contest was on.

Accordingly, the prophets of Baal took their bull and prepared the sacrifice. From morning until noon they prayed in the name of Baal, shouting, "O Baal, answer us!" (v. 26). But there was no sound or any response. Then they began to do a crazy-looking half-limp, half-dance around the altar, a special spiritual effect designed to catch the attention of their god. All this kept on until noon, at which time Elijah showed his full-fledged humanity. He began to taunt them: "Cry louder to your god. Maybe he is meditating" (see v. 27).

Carried away with the promise of victory, Elijah showed his humanity and acted like a football fan ahead by twenty-one points at halftime. After Elijah's taunts the prophets of Baal shifted into a frenzy trying to get Baal's attention. They cried louder and louder; they gashed themselves with swords and spears until the blood flowed. But there was no response from Baal.

Then Elijah said to the people, "Come in closer." He built up the altar with twelve stones, representing the twelve sons of Jacob, and laid the bull on the wood. Then, so that the people would be even more impressed with the miracle, Elijah dug a trench around the altar and commanded someone to fill four large jars of water and douse the bull, not once but three times, until the altar area looked like a swimming pool. He didn't want some little stunt that Jezebel's professors could explain away; he wanted a full-blown miracle.

Then he prayed, "Answer me, Yahweh, answer me, so that this people may know that you, Yahweh, are God, and that as you let them go from you it is yours also to bring them back."[4]

Then the fire of Yahweh struck the altar, the offering was consumed in flames, and when the people saw it they fell on their faces and cried: "[Yahweh], he is God; [Yahweh], he is God" (v. 39).

That is what Elijah's name in Hebrew means: "Yahweh is God."

Then with the rush of victory running through his veins and in obedience to the Law of Yahweh (Deut. 13:6,9) that false prophets be put to death, Elijah said: "Seize the prophets of Baal; do not let one of them escape." Then Scripture records, "They seized them; and Elijah took them down to the wadi Kishon, and he slaughtered them there" (v. 40, *The Jerusalem Bible*).

It is not a pretty scene. We cringe at the violence. We like our politics bloody, but not our religion. But maybe our religion is not much different than our politics. Virtually every war ever fought has been called by each side a "holy war."

But we this day who gather in Christ's name have a deeper glimpse of truth; we have a higher revelation that judges both this text and us. It is the revelation of Jesus Christ. He disavowed the violence of revenge.

Elijah was before Christ; however, these were the rules of ancient Israel, and the victory of Yahweh was sealed in blood.

God had acted; the people did choose; and the flame of Yahweh which had been flickering like a spent candle now flamed brightly.

Why?

Because His people stopped limping between two opinions and followed Yahweh.

Because His people stopped hopping on one foot and then the other and placed both feet in service of Yahweh.

Because His people discovered they couldn't worship two masters and chose the only One who counts.

Elijah, part 1, ends with an unforgettable scene. God had won the victory at Mount Carmel, and now our attention is turned to the crisis which began the story—the drought. There had been no rain for three and a half years; the land was parched and barren. Now, according to God's promise, the drought ends.

Listen to how this dramatic chapter in Elijah's life ends.

Elijah said to Ahab, "Get moving, it's about to rain" (see v. 41). Elijah then climbed to the top of Mount Carmel and crouched down on the ground with his face between his knees.

To his young servant he said, "Go up and look out to the sea." The servant went and looked. "There is nothing at all" (vv. 43-44, *The Jerusalem Bible*). he said. Seven times Elijah sent him to look. On the seventh time the boy reported, "Yes, I can see—a cloud no bigger than a man's hand rising up out of the sea." Elijah said, "Go tell Ahab" (see vv. 44-45). And as he went the sky grew dark, the winds came, and then the rain, sweet heavy rain.

And Elijah ran in front of the chariot, seventeen miles he ran, all the way back to Jezreel. After all that, you could have, too.

Notes

1. Davie Napier, *Word of God, Word of Earth* (Philadelphia: United Church Press, 1976). These are his Beecher Lectures based upon the Elijah cycle.
2. Frederick Buechner, *Peculiar Treasures* (New York: Harper & Row, 1979), p. 9.
3. Napier, p. 28.
4. Davie Napier's translation of 1 Kings 18:37, p. 37.

Additional Bibliography

F. W. Krummacher, *Elijah the Tishbite* (Grand Rapids: Baker Book House, reprinted 1977). This is a brilliant precritical exposition of the Elijah cycle.

7
Elijah, 2

Elijah had just come from one of the most dramatic victories of God in all history. Remember? The contest at Mount Carmel, the two altars. The challenge to the prophets of Baal: you put a bull on your altar, I'll put a bull on mine. If Baal lights your sacrifice, he is God; If Yahweh God lights my sacrifice, He is God. And then the challenge to the people: "If [Yahweh] be God, follow him, but if Baal, then follow him" (1 Kings 18:21, KJV). Baal was silent, but Yahweh rained down fire from heaven and the sacrifice went up in flames.

It was one of the most dramatic examples of God's visible power in all the Bible. It is glorious to follow God when God acts so openly, so plainly on behalf of His people.

But today's half of the story could not be more different. We see a truer test of faithfulness. It is easy to be faithful when God is speaking, but what if God is silent? It is easy to have faith when God is acting, but what if God does nothing? It is easy to believe when God is present, but what if God is absent?

We have gone to Mount Carmel with Elijah where God acts in such a visible and dramatic way we feel that anyone would be a fool not to believe in God. Now we go with the same prophet, Elijah, to Mount Horeb, where God is silent; and we wonder if anybody but a fool could believe in God.

The last half of the story is set in three places: the juniper tree, Mount Horeb, and Naboth's Vineyard.

Heading for the juniper tree.—When Ahab arrived from Mount Carmel at Jezreel he told Jezebel all that had happened: the contest, Baal's impotence, Yahweh's power, Elijah's slaughtering of all Baal's prophets, and the end of the long drought—just as Elijah had said it would end. Ahab trembled in excitement. The true God had shown His power, and His name was not Baal but Yahweh!

But Jezebel's face blackened with rage. She swore to avenge the death of her prophets with the death of Elijah. Within twenty-four hours she said she would have his head.

She sent the death threat to Elijah. The words were short, but Elijah got the point.

"If you are Elijah, I am Jezebel."[1] Get the point? "You may be a prophet, but I am the queen." You've gotten the message before. You disobeyed your parents and the moment of reckoning comes: "You may be Steve, but I am your father." You get a paper back at school and you have to do it over: "If you are a student, I am teacher." You get a termination notice at work: "You may be an employee, but I am the boss." Or you pretend you're still a teenager and play a game of softball. The next day your body says: Your name is John, but my name is middle age. "If you are Elijah, then I am Jezebel." Elijah got the point.

If Elijah's humanity showed itself earlier when he taunted the prophets of Baal, it also showed itself now in fear and despair. The text says: "Frightened for his life, he ran away" (see 19:3). And where he ran was to a juniper tree.

The juniper tree.—Trembling in fear, heavy with despair, and overcome in self-pity, Elijah sat under the juniper tree. But Elijah did not pray some polite prayer from some $2.95 prayer book he picked up in the grocery store. He came clean with God and lifted his complaint to God: "It is enough" (v. 4). I've had it, Yahweh. Take my life. You don't need me. I'm no better than anybody else.

Elijah was terrified and in despair. He had thought Mount Carmel's dramatic victory would turn the tide and ensure the success of Yahweh and his champion prophet Elijah. But just the reverse happened. The powers of evil intensified; Jezebel was out to kill him; and a people who need Mount Carmels in order to believe do not long stay faithful.

Who of us has not felt like Elijah, sitting under the juniper tree, discouraged, depressed, ready to throw in the towel? Who has not felt like praying: "Yahweh, Eternal God, enough! I've had it. I've had all the Jezebels I can stand. I've had enough of gutless wonders like Ahab, enough of wishy-washy worshipers of Thine; I've had a stomachful of this sorry world where evil prospers and the good die young, good men like yours truly. And I can't do anything about it. I want out, I've had enough. Take my life, or what's left of it. Jezebel can have me! Who wants to live anyway?"

Or perhaps you've sat under the juniper tree of sickness or sadness, of failure or doubt. You feel like the weight of darkness is too heavy to carry. It all makes so little sense. We are afraid to pray for fear God will not answer. Afraid *not* to pray, we blurt out our need to God. We sit under the juniper tree and say with Elijah, "It is enough; I've just about had it." For you who now sit under such a tree, know that you do not sit alone. There is One beside you who under the shadow of another tree called Calvary cried, "My God, my God, why hast thou forsaken me?" (Matt. 27:46).

But note what happened next. Elijah went to sleep. As he slept, "someone" came, woke him up, and said, "Wake up and eat." He looked up and there was a biscuit and some water. With new strength he traveled on to Mount Horeb.

Who woke up and fed him? The earliest traditions simply record that "someone" did. We may wonder if the "someone" was an angel of God. Well, an angel this someone *was* who fed and cared for him. The deepest and darkest of our most ultimate questioning is not answered by a doctoral dissertation; it is answered by a hand on the shoulder, a plate of food, a glass of water. In the thick darkness of despondency, in the cold sweat of fear, "someone" comes from God to wake us, feed us, and care for us. God sends

His own to take care of His own. Remember the moments in your life when an "angel" has come, in a phone call, in a cup of coffee over the breakfast table, in any number of simple ways. Even when we give up on God, God does not give up on us. He sends "someone." And, with that unexpected help, we, like Elijah, go on.

Mount Horeb.—Where did Elijah go but to Mount Horeb, the other name for Mount Sinai! Still shaken, fearful, unsure, Elijah went to the holy mountain of God where Moses received the Ten Commandments, the holy mountain of God where amid wind, earthquake, and fire God had made Himself known.

Elijah came to this sacred place hoping for a repeat performance, for some dramatic sign that Yahweh was still God, that Mount Carmel was no fluke, that he, Elijah, was still God's prophet. He came for some reassurance, for an instant replay of revelation, for something to hang onto. Elijah climbed the mountain and lodged in a cave.

What happened next is one of those holy moments of history. We bow our hearts and minds before it. In the stark simplicity of the language, here is what happened:

> And there was a mighty wind
> Not in the wind was Yahweh
>
> And after the wind, an earthquake
> Not in the earthquake was Yahweh
>
> And after the earthquake, a fire
> Not in the fire was Yahweh
>
> And after the fire—
> A sound of utmost silence.[1]

Imagine! There Elijah was, hoping for God to reveal himself in the wind, just like the wind that had parted the Red Sea for Moses, but the wind came and God was not there; hoping for God to speak in the earthquake like the one that shook the mountain when God gave Moses the Ten Commandments, but the earthquake came and no God, no new Law, nothing; hoping for God to reveal himself through fire, just as he led Moses and His people through the wilderness with a pillar of fire, just as He had rained down fire at Mount Carmel, but the fire came and God was not there.

All the ways through which God had revealed himself were now empty. God was not there. Imagine the terror of the moment. Have you had times like that when God does not seem to be acting as He once did? The old words don't mean anything. You sing the hymns, but they no longer move you. Sermons seem vain and void. You come and go to church, but the feeling is not there. Prayers seem to never go higher than the ceiling. The symbols are empty. It seems as though God has turned His back. Not in the wind, not in the earthquake, not in the fire, not in prayers, not in worship, not in church; God is not there.

When we experience this we go through the "dark night of the soul." A crisis of faith is at hand. Our choice is: do we go on listening, hoping, waiting upon the Lord, or do we call it quits?

What the Scriptures record next gives us hope in the darkness.

"And after the fire—a sound of utmost silence. And . . . Elijah covered his face with his robe" (see 19:13).

God was there—in the silence. "The still small voice" is the translation that rings in our ears, but there was no voice. The Hebrew words are a poet's words: the sound of crushed silence, a hush, utter quiet. But God was *there;* unexplainable, unexplained, God was there.

And Elijah knew it and, overcome by the Presence, covered his face with his robe.

Faith is not really faith until the darkness, until the silence of God. There are those times when God turns His back, when He is silent. Perhaps He needs to move from one way of acting to another and must empty the old modes of His presence so we will look for the new ways. Perhaps we have so abused His words and His symbols that He becomes silent, so that we will once again hunger for His righteousness. Perhaps He can do no more than weep, and we will not allow Him to weep, just as we will not allow Him to laugh, so we hear nothing but silence.

The mystery is deep. We can only ask questions and talk about our side, the human side of God's silence which is faith.

Faith is the patience to hang in there when all seems wrong, when days come and go and God seems strangely absent. Faith is

waiting for God when God no longer comes as of old. Faith is keeping the eyes and ears open, to hear and see when God does come:
> not in sounds
> but in silence
> not in action
> but in stillness
> not as of old
> but as of *now.*

Give us, O God, the faith to see Thy new Advent, Thy coming to us in ways not seen before.

Elijah did not get signs and wonders; Elijah did not get answers; Elijah waited and got in the crushed silence God's Presence. And that, after all, is what we need most—not signs and wonders, not answers, but God Himself.

The absence of God in the wind, earthquake, and fire created the crisis of faith necessary for Elijah to look for God anew, to wait for Him and to watch. Silence is the beginning of prayer. The silence of God evokes from us new yearning for him! And from our yearning new faith is born. "Blessed are those who hunger and thirst for righteousness," Jesus said, "for they shall be satisfied" (Matt. 5:6). "If with all your hearts ye truly seek him, ye shall truly find him," is Jeremiah's promise in that gorgeous solo from Mendelssohn's *Elijah.*

God's absence in the traditional forms caused Elijah to look for God and find Him in the silences. And now the way was prepared for a whole new way of knowing God and serving God. We have at Mount Horeb but another transition moment in the history of faith. From now on we see God working not through wind, earthquake, and fire, but through people. God was absenting Himself from nature to force us to see Him acting in history. It was the birth of the prophetic vision. God moves from "nature in tumult" to "the tempests of the soul,"[3] from the wonder of theophany to the hope of theocracy. Having defeated Baal on Mount Carmel, God now moves the contest itself to the human struggle for righteousness and mercy.

From the silence in the cave came the voice of Yahweh who, now, for the first time in this encounter, spoke: "What are you doing here, Elijah?" (19:13). Elijah went through his carefully planned speech: "Lord, I have been a fanatic for Thee and all the while your people have thrown down the altars and killed your prophets. I alone am left and now they are after *me*. That's why I'm here" (see v. 14).

And God then spoke His word. It came in the twin graces of *recommissioning* and *reassurance*.

First the grace of the new call. He said, "Elijah, get off this mountain. I've got some work for you to do: anoint Hazael king of Damascus, anoint Jehu king of Israel, and anoint Elisha as your successor" (see vv. 15-16). God was calling him to the work of a prophet, the first great prophet, God's spokesperson in the affairs of the world, a world living under the sovereignty of God.

And now the grace of *reassurance*. It was at the same time the gift of *community*. It was a word of good news that corrected Elijah's cynicism and gave him hope. Some of us live by the slogan: "He serves best who merely sits and complains." But God won't let us do that for long.

He said to Elijah: "Elijah, go on back to your people. You're not the only believer left. There are seven thousand left in Israel whose knees have never bent to Baal, nor whose lips have kissed him" (see v. 18).

Sometimes we, too, lose heart, and God tells us: "Don't give up. Listen, there are thousands out there on my side working alongside you."

While it could be wrong to look too favorably on our times, it is also an error to look too gloomily.

The reach and strength of God's kingdom is far greater than we can see. Jesus said, "The kingdom of God cometh not with observation" (Luke 17:20, KJV). And God has many people secretly at work for Him—inside and outside the church.

We worry about the lack of true preachers, but God has promised where shepherds are corrupt to take charge of the flock Himself.

We decry the lack of honest people in high places, but there are always Obadiahs in the courts of Ahab. Obadiah was a priest in Ahab's court. While Ahab was trying to kill all God's prophets, Obadiah was hiding a hundred of them in caves and feeding them!

We moan over the lack of courage in our witness, but Jesus said, "If you don't tell the good news, the very stones of the earth will cry it out" (see Luke 19:40). The kingdom of God is the kingdom of *God* and He is marching on!

Go back to the real world, Elijah, and get busy. There are seven thousand back there who have not bowed their knees to Baal.

So back he went, recommissioned and reassured, with a call and a community. The prophetic vision was born.

Naboth's vineyard.—The last scene is in Naboth's vineyard. It is a confrontation between Ahab and Elijah.

Ahab wanted a pretty piece of property adjoining his. The problem was that Naboth, the owner of the vineyard, refused to sell. Naboth was one of those seven thousand! When Naboth refused, Ahab went into a *sulk*. Sullen and seething, he went to bed and refused to eat.

When Jezebel asked him why he was sulking and he told her, she replied, "Who is king—you or Naboth? Are you a man or a mouse, 'a king or a cup of custard?' "4 Jezebel proceeded to have Naboth framed and executed and gave Ahab the vineyard for a present.

Ahab went to take possession of the vineyard. While he was on the way the Word of Yahweh came to Elijah and told him to deliver this message to Ahab: "Having murdered, do you even now take possession? In the place where the dogs licked Naboth's blood they shall lick your blood" (see 21:19).

Elijah met Ahab in Naboth's vineyard. Ahab said to Elijah: "Have you found me, O my enemy?" Elijah replied, "I have found you" (v. 20).

With that last confrontation Elijah closed out his work. As was prophesied, Ahab and Jezebel went to their grisly deaths. Elijah the prophet proved the truth: "The grass withers, the flower fades; but the word of our God will stand forever" (Isa.40:8). In that hope we live.

But hope lies in yet another place as well. Elijah did not taste death as only a mortal man but was taken up into heaven amid a whirlwind. That passage points to another hope, a resurrection hope that Another would come and conquer death as a preview of things to come. Maybe the two hopes together—a hope in the word of God that endures forever and hope in life that lies beyond this world—are why Elijah is called "the Prophet," and why Malachi prophesied that Elijah would appear again, preparing the way for the Messiah. Maybe that is why every year at the Passover meal the Jews leave a door open for Elijah's return and set a place at the table for him. Only a prophet who saw God in the lightning on Mount Carmel and who waited for God in the silence of Mount Horeb can prepare us for the One who came hidden in human flesh and for that great day when our Messiah will return in power and glory and open up heaven's door.

Notes

1. I am grateful to Davie Napier for his translation and exposition of this passage, *Word of God, Word of Earth* (Philadelphia: United Church Press, 1976), p. 58 ff.
2. This translation is a variation of Davie Napier, p. 56.
3. Samuel Terrien, *The Elusive Presence: Toward a New Biblical Theology* (San Francisco: Harper & Row, 1978), p. 229.
4. Frederick Buechner's phrase, *Peculiar Treasures* (New York: Harper & Row, 1979), p. 10.

8
Amos

If the prophetic vision was born with Elijah in the silence of God at Mount Horeb, it came to full flower in the prophet Amos. Amos was among the classical prophets of Israel, the writing prophets.

As I have said before, the Old Testament prophets were not so much foretellers as forthtellers; they spoke *forth* God's Word. "The prophets unveiled not the future but the absolute."[1] The prophets were predictors of the Messiah, but more, they were among the first who dreamed God's dream of a Messiah. The prophets are often thought of as social reformers, and that, of course, they were; but they were more than social reformers. The prophets were, in Samuel Terrien's words, *"poets of divine presence."*[2] They had received, to quote Longfellow, "the prophet's vision,/The exultation, the divine/Insanity of noble minds."[3]

The prophets of ancient Israel were captivated by God's righteous presence; through them God's ideal of a righteous nation was held high. People called them insane, but their madness was the "insanity of noble minds."

Amos was the mouthpiece of God the Lion. "The Lord roars from Zion" (1:2), Amos said. When Amos defended his call he said, I was minding my own business as a shepherd when "God kidnapped me from behind my flock."[4] Like some lamb seized by a mountain lion, I was seized by God's word. "The lion has roared, who will not fear?" said Amos. "The Lord God has spoken; who can but prophesy?" (3:8). Amos roared with the roar of God the lion.

His first, and perhaps last, sermon was an unforgettable scene. It was the most high and holy day for the nation of Israel: the yearly celebration at Bethel. On this day the people worshiped at the shrine of civil religion. It was a mixing of patriotism and religion. The state and church joined arms to sing "God bless our Israel." They had good reason to be happy. This occurred in eighth-century Israel, at the height of military strength and economic prosperity that the Northern Kingdom would ever reach. Jereboam II was rating high marks in the polls and Wall Street was happy.

This yearly celebration at Bethel was like inauguration day in America. The president was there; so were the priests and the poets, the music and the prayers.

Now, in the middle of the ceremony, in walked an unknown, poorly dressed migrant farmer. Part of the year he tended a poor man's variety of sheep in the desert fringe. Then he moved north where he pinched back sycamore trees and then headed south again to herd a scrawny type of oxen. Known only as "Amos [of the] shepherds of Tekoa" (1:1), perhaps an orphan, now a poor migrant farmer, in he walked and announced an unforgettable message from God.

The crowd was confused and nervous at first—what would this rude intruder say? But soon their anxiety gave way to approval and applause. For Amos began announcing God's judgment on the *enemies* of Israel. (That will preach!) Thus says the Lord:

"For the sins of Damascus I will punish them," says the Lord.

"Amen," went the senators.

"For the sins of Gaza I will destroy them."

"Amen," went the judges.

"For the sins of Tyre I will send proper punishments."

"Amen," cried the lobbyists.

"For the sins of Edom and Ammon I will repay," says the Lord.

"Amen," cried the whole crowd, breaking into spontaneous applause. "This preacher may be a bit scruffy-looking, but he knows how to *preach!*"

Then as they leaned forward, licking their lips in anticipation for the next denunciation from the Lord, Amos let them have it between the eyes.

"For the sins of Israel, for *your* sins, God will punish *you.*"

In stunned silence, the crowd listened. Amos went on: "You sell your righteousness for cash. You buy and sell the needy for a measly pair of sandals. You trample the heads of the poor into the dust. You vote your pocketbook."

Then he looked out at the sea of $10,000 gowns, top hats, and tuxedos and said: "You lie on ivory beds while people are cold and lonely."

He looked at the overnourished women and said: "You cows of Bashan, you sit around and say 'Bring me more to drink,' while people starve" (see 4:1-3).

He turned to the judges and said: "Your courts of law are a sham. The famous and rich get preferential treatment; the poor and forgotten get no justice at all."

He said: "*You've been crooked so long you don't know what straight is.* Let me show you a straight line. I saw the Lord in a dream. He was standing beside a wall built with a plumb line with a plumb line in his hand. He said, "Amos, what do you see?" I said, "A plumb line," and He said, "This plumb line I now set in the midst of my people."

Only God's Word can set us straight.

Then Amos turned to the religious folk in the crowd, the preachers and the churchgoers, and gave an even harder word. "This is what God has to say to you: You come to church and use my name, but you ignore the needs of your neighbor. You have religion, but you don't have love.

For that reason I despise your covered-dish suppers and worship services. When you take up offerings I turn my head; you sing hymns but they are like noise to my ears.

Here is what I want: 'Let justice roll down like waters, and righteousness like an everflowing stream' " (5:24).

God was saying what He would say again and again through his prophets: I don't want lavish ceremony; I want right living.

Sydney Harris recently wrote a comment that evoked bushels of negative mail. He said: "God could do well with less praise from his children and more imitation." That word was no more popular than Amos's word.

Here is what concerns God most: not elaborate ritual, not even perfect doctrine, but right living. Not ortho*doxy*, but ortho*praxy*.

"Let justice roll down like waters, and righteousness like an everflowing stream."

"Like waters, . . . like an everflowing stream." A remarkable image. God's justice and righteousness are the life-giving streams of society. They replenish the barren land. Like an everflowing stream they must come—not like the floodwaters that periodically wash in and rush over a parched land, causing ruin, never soaking into the ground, but like an everflowing stream.[5]

Implicit in the image is a warning of judgment. Like an everflowing stream God's justice must flow. When we block up the flowing waters of justice with the dam of our greed, prejudice, and selfishness, then the earth begins to wither. The waters heap up dark and furious against the walls of the dam until finally they break through, destroying the dam, the torrential waters pouring over the land causing destruction. When this happens, God's justice has become judgment and His righteousness has turned into wrath.

"Like an everflowing stream." God needs more than ritualistic kindness: fruit baskets at Christmas. Along with charity, God wants justice. A Christmas bonus is no substitute for a living wage.

"Let justice roll down like waters, and righteousness like an everflowing stream."

Remember a few years back when the media publicized the famine in Central Africa? Our compassion moved us to send thousands of tons of grain, such huge quantities in such a short span of time that the grain spoiled and rotted in the loading docks.

Justice needs to be like rolling waters, like an everflowing stream.

What is justice; what is righteousness? Naming them is risky *and* necessary.

A life lived by the Ten Commandments, personal morality, racial justice, equal rights for women, fairness in the courts, protection for the weak and disabled, opportunity for honest work: these are the marks of God's righteousness. They need far more than occasional guilt-ridden splurges of concern. They need constant, patient, and persistent concern, like an everflowing stream.

These words from God are not easy words. In fact, they got even harder. Amos said, "You talk about the future 'day of the Lord,' when the Lord God will come to earth and fix things. You think God will defend you and judge your enemies. Instead it will be a day of darkness for you because you have ignored God's ethical demands. 'Woe to you who desire the day of the Lord' (v. 18). You will be like a man running from a lion and running headlong into a bear (v. 19)."

The same word can be spoken to those today who talk glibly about a "Rapture" and speak of how glorious it is that we Christians will escape the "Tribulation" God has planned for our enemies, all the while ignoring God's justice and righteousness. "You may have a surprise in store," warned Amos.

Amos had another vision; it was of a basket of ripe summer fruit. You are ripe, about to spoil, Amos told the people. You are that basket of ripe fruit.

Then came the darkest prophecy of all. All Amos's words were hard words—just as some of Jesus' words were hard. But there is something far worse than hearing the hard word of a just God—it is hearing nothing at all.

Amos said, There is a famine coming that is much worse than a famine of steaks and grain, much worse than a shortage of oil and gas.

"Behold the days are coming," says the Lord God, "When I will send a famine on the land; not a famine of bread, nor a thirst for water, but of hearing the words of the Lord" (8:11).

The final price of disobedience is this: that God will make His word so scarce that no one will be able to find it, so scarce, in Buechner's words, "that the world won't even know what it is starving to death *for*."6

As you can guess, Amos did not become the king's favorite preacher. He was not invited to the White House to preach. In the seventh chapter of Amos we have a comic confrontation between Amos and the king's priest Amaziah. Amaziah sent a message to king Jereboam saying, "Amos has conspired against you . . . the land is not able to bear all his words" (7:10). Truer words were never spoken. Sometimes we cannot bear God's Word, but neither can we afford to ignore it.

Then Amaziah confronted Amos face to face and invited him to leave: "O [man of visions go back to] Judah and . . . prophesy there [Love thy neighbor—send him your prophets]; but never again prophesy at Bethel, for it is the king's sanctuary" (vv. 12-13). Prophets rarely belong in kings' sanctuaries. A book a few years ago was entitled *Sermons Not Preached at the White House.* Amos's sermon belonged there.

Amos replied, "I am no prophet or son of a prophet. I am not here by profession or by choice. I am a shepherd, a pincher of sycamore trees. I was minding my own business, tending my flock, when God Almighty kidnapped me from behind my flock. Like some sheep seized by a mountain lion I was seized by the Word of God. The lion roars, and I can do no other than roar along with him" (see v. 14).

With that Amos was thrown out of Bethel. Most likely he then went underground back to the south, where he wrote down his visions and spoke to a small group of followers, two of whom might have been a man named Hosea and a younger fellow named Isaiah.

For the Northern Kingdom of Israel, Amos was God's last call to repent. "Seek the Lord and live! " Amos pleaded. "Let justice roll down like waters, and righteousness like an everflowing stream."

But the people did not repent. And the waters of God's justice and righteousness heaped up dark and furious against the walls of their stubbornness, until the waters broke over the dam of their sins, justice turned to judgment, and the Northern Kingdom fell to the Assyrians.

The nation of Israel fell as all nations have fallen, not from without but from within. The inner decay of a people who will not hear God's Word is the destruction of a nation. All an outside nation does is mop up what's left.

Conclusion

The lion still roars. Jesus did not abolish the Law and the Prophets; He fulfilled them. The kingdom of God has to do not only with the finding and losing of souls but also the finding and losing of nations. It has to do with a person who meets the living Christ and accepts Him as Savior and Lord, and it has to do with a nation choosing to live by God's standards. The nation's only hope is to live under the "righteousing" power of God.

God is not mocked. If justice does not flow like waters, it turns to judgment. If righteousness does not roll like an everflowing stream, it turns to wrath. "Let justice roll down like waters, and righteousness like an everflowing stream."

Everyone in this nation, "Seek the Lord and live!"

Notes

1. Samuel Terrien, *The Elusive Presence* (San Francisco: Harper & Row, 1978), p. 227.
2. Ibid.
3. Cited in Terrien, p. 227.
4. Terrien's translation of 7:15, p. 236.
5. See Martin Buber, *The Prophetic Faith* (New York: Harper & Row Torchbook, 1960), p. 100 ff.
6. Frederick Buechner, *Peculiar Treasures* (New York: Harper & Row, 1979), p. 11.

9
Hosea

"Love is blind," they say. Maybe that is how Hosea and Gomer got married. They were as unlikely a couple as you've ever seen. She, Gomer, was a flower child with an easy smile and a devil-may-care disposition. He, Hosea, was a preacher with what could be called an inconsistent personality. His psychiatrist friends told him he was a manic-depressive. He said, "Well, then, I'm a manic-depressive for the Lord! It is the Word of God that determines my disposition. When the Lord is angry, I'm angry. When he is sad, I'm sad. When he is happy, then I'll be happy, too." Obviously his rough edges had not yet been smoothed by clinical pastoral education.

How the two, Hosea and Gomer, met is anybody's guess. Maybe she came down the aisle at a revival service. Maybe they met on the street; he, a street preacher; she, a street person. Somehow or other they met. Maybe the opposites attracted; perhaps the hunger in each of their souls found a hint of solace in the difference they found in the other. Who knows? How unsearchable are the ways of the human heart. Anyway, for whatever reasons, they met and were married.

We don't know when the cracks began to show in the marriage. The first child was named *Jezreel,* which was in itself a sermon of judgment. Jezreel was the infamous place of some pretty messy political doings. Imagine a preacher naming his firstborn son *Watergate*—just to remind the people of its sins. Can you imagine Gomer going along with that?!

Hosea

"Hosea, what will the other children say when they hear his name at school? They'll laugh."

"God's not laughing," Hosea retorted. "It's no laughing matter what this country is coming to. God gave me the name. End of discussion."

What could Gomer say? Married to a man of God, or maybe he was what the people were saying about him in the streets: "The prophet is a fool/the man of the spirit is mad" (9:7).

What an odd couple: she, laid back and easy, he, God's workaholic. She with the easy smile. He a manic-depressive for the Lord—mostly depressive. "No, I don't need Lithium," he would tell the doctors. "This *country* needs to change—that's all. Then I'd be happy—and so would God."

Then came the second child, a girl. He named her *Lo-ruhamah*, which means "Not-Loved." Not so inappropriate a name for a middle child, you might be saying. But the name might have signaled darker things. "Not-Loved." Why? One scholar has translated the name this way: "She-that-Never-Knew-a-Father's-Love." Was there the suggestion that the child was not his? That conclusion seems justified by the time the third child was born. This one was named *Lo-Ammi:* "Not-My-People or Not-My-Kin." It was the kind of name more normally yelled at the umpire than spoken at church, the kind more apt to be found on a bathroom wall than in a Sunday School periodical.

Gomer had taken up with other men; and, as Frederick Buechner put it, "any resemblance between her next batch of children and Hosea was purely coincidental."[1]

Those first six years of marriage must have been torment for the both of them. Many times Hosea must have wondered why he had ever married Gomer, and Gomer surely wondered the same.

As Hosea went round and round inside his head as to the whys of it all, the answer came as a word from the Lord. *"Go take for yourself a wife of harlotry,"* was the word. "But, Lord," Hosea argued, "I didn't know she was like that."

"Go take for yourself a wife of harlotry and have children of

harlotry.' "Lord, you and the whole town know that. How can I take what they are all saying behind my back?"

"Go take for yourself a wife of harlotry and have children of harlotry, for the land commits great harlotry by forsaking the Lord" (see 1:2).

That was it. The image seared Hosea's mind and heart. Through the suffering of his own marriage, Hosea was given a window into the heart of God. God Himself was the husband, and Israel, His beloved, had gone whoring after false gods. Hosea's marriage then was transformed into a living word of God to his people.

A bad marriage became the medium of divine revelation. But we should not be surprised—so was the dishonesty of Jacob, the adultery of David, the prejudice of Jonah, and even the cross where Jesus hung and died.

So the marriage became the medium of God's word to Israel. It was a word of judgment and suffering love. It transfigured the common understanding of sin. Sin was more than disobedience; it was infidelity. Sin does more than break rules; it breaks hearts—even God's heart. The relationship of God to His people is as intimate as that between husband and wife. God is ever wooing us into His arms. And when we turn from Him we do more than break laws; we break relationship with Him.

The marriage became a living parable of the infidelity of Israel. It was at one level a *political infidelity.* Israel had left Yahweh and sought the favors of Assyria and Egypt. Unwilling to trust in the strength of the Lord, Israel sought security in the chariots of Assyria or in warriors of Egypt. So God's word came: "You are like a half-baked piece of dough; you are like a silly dove flitting from Assyria to Egypt; you are like a prostitute who has to pay her lovers; you are like a man getting more and more gray hairs, but refusing to see he is growing old" (see 7:8-12). But all of the images found their deeper sense in the dominant symbol of the marriage: you are like a wife taking other lovers.

And this infidelity was also manifest in *social corruption.* "[I] see swearing, lying, killing, stealing, and committing adultery;

... murder follows murder," God said (4:2). Hosea saw the same social sickness that Amos saw: the poor got poorer and the rich got richer. God wanted justice, but what He got was a cry of distress.

But Hosea's vision went deeper than that of Amos. Sin was more than breaking laws; it was infidelity. And the root of sin is the heart—the heart filled with the spirit of harlotry. So at the root of the political corruption and social injustice and immorality was *spiritual infidelity.*

Israel had left Yahweh and gone seeking other lovers: the baalim, all the gods of Baal religion. Baal religion was the religion of fertility. The people believed that when Baal wedded himself to the land, then the weather would be good and bumper crops would ensue. So to incite the sexual yearning of Baal, they practiced ritual prostitution. Drunken orgies around the altar would ensure that Baal would mate himself to the land and guarantee a bumper crop of wheat, barley, goats, and babies.

Many in Israel left Yahweh and went to Baal. Yahweh talked of righteousness and Baal talked of the bottom line—the crop report. Given the choice, most chose Baal. Baal promised vitality through sexual excitement. Yahweh promised wholeness through covenant love. Given the choice, most of us would choose Baal.

But infidelity to Yahweh was enacted in more subtle ways. Outwardly they still worshiped, but inwardly they turned Yahweh into Baal. It was *"the baalization of Yahweh."*[2] They still said, "Lord, Lord"; but their "Lord" was but a projection of baser wishes. And so we transform our God into projections of our wishes, the Americanization of God, God packaged by Madison Avenue, the God of success, sensuality, and self.

Hosea looked at Israel and saw *spiritual corruption:* he saw priests robbing people; he saw people offering sacrifices in the shade, the "comfortable pew." He saw careless repentance. He saw people going through the motions of offering sacrifices but ignoring the claims of justice and the needs of the poor and helpless.

So all Hosea could see was judgment for Israel. "[You] sow the wind," he said, "and [you will] reap the whirlwind" (8:7). But perhaps the most terrifying thing of all was what he saw sin doing to the hearts of the people. Sin was destroying the hearts of the people. They no longer even had the desire to return to the Lord. The more they sinned the further they drifted from Yahweh until they lost all will to return to Yahweh. "Wine and whoredom have taken away the heart," said the Lord (see 4:11). The spirit of harlotry has led you astray until you no longer even desire to come home to God. Your will is in bondage. You are no longer free even to repent!"

That was the deep sorrow of God. It was also the deep sorrow of Hosea when he returned home one day and found the note from Gomer. She was gone again, this time for good. She had left what seemed like a hundred times before, always returning repentant and sorry. But this time there would be no return. She was through with him. She no longer had any desire to stay married to Hosea.

So what was Hosea to do? Divorce her, lick his wounds, begin to pick his life up, and go on? He had nearly raised the children himself. That would not be much of a change. The divorce would be easy. The grounds were clear.

Then came the moment, the moment no one could have anticipated. And Hosea's story, God's story, your story and mine have not been the same since.

God came again to Hosea and said, *"Go again, and love [this woman who has a lover] and is an adulteress"* (see 3:1). So Hosea went out and searched for her. He found her enslaved in some prostitution ring, perhaps the ritual prostitution racket of Baal, perhaps just the street variety we know today. He bought off her contract, paid for her freedom, and took her home again.

And that was what happened to God in his relationship with Israel, too. The divine anguish of God does not turn to angry judgment. Instead, it turns to a suffering love that will not let us go.

> How can I give you up, O Ephraim!
> How can I hand you over, O Israel!

> My heart recoils within me,
>   my compassion grows warm and tender.
> I will not execute my fierce anger,
>
> for I am God and not man,
>   the Holy One in your midst,
>   and I will not come to destroy (11:8-9).

The images come flooding from the heart of God. Though you suffer the consequences of your sin, I will come bandage your wounds. Though you bring judgment on yourselves, I will come and heal you (6:1-2). Though divorce is what you deserve, I will not give up on you.

You will again call me "My Husband" rather than "My Baal"; and I, Yahweh, will call you "my bride." I will betroth you to me forever. I will betroth you in righteousness and in justice, in steadfast love, mercy and faithfulness (see 2:16-20).

God's story with His people became Hosea's story as well. The reconciliation reached all the way to the children and their names. Those names once given as judgment now became signs of mercy. The child *Jezreel* will sow goodness instead of judgment. Hosea will love *Not Loved* until she is called *Much Loved* and he will say to his child *Not My People,* "You Are My People, You Are My Child."

In this story of Hosea and Gomer, God's heart of hearts is unveiled for us in a way never seen before. God will never stop loving us. While we bring judgment on ourselves, God is ever ready to bind our wounds and take us home.

But there can be no such love without suffering. Such is the cross in the heart of God, active in every moment of His history with us and made inescapably plain on a Roman cross. Our infidelity cannot stop God from loving us, but it turns His love into a suffering love.

Can you imagine the cost of such a love to Hosea? There was no guarantee that Gomer would be his and his alone even after he bought her freedom and brought her home. We are not told the end of the story. Such is the cost of love that will not coerce. And can you imagine the cost of that kind of love to God? It cost Him His son, yet He still comes after us with His love.

However, the prophet Hosea does more than articulate the pain of suffering love. He also envisions its final victory. By the power and grace of God, suffering love will finally become a triumphant love. Hosea lived in the hope that a patient love, eloquent in its suffering, can change the human heart and bring reconciliation. "I will heal their faithfulness," says the Lord, "I will love them freely"; and God's wayward people "shall return and dwell beneath my shadow" (14:4,7). We all live in that hope, with that prayer, by that promise.

A question has hounded me as I have delved into the story of Hosea: Are we, the church, Hosea, or are we Gomer?

Are we Gomer, the faithless wife whom God the husband keeps on loving? Are we the world God so loves? And I answer, yes, we are Gomer, we are the bride of Christ whom Christ loved and gave Himself for. Though we flirt with other lovers, Christ will not forsake us. We are the forgiven people of God. God is forever saying to us: "Though you take up with other lovers, I will not give up on you. Though you live as if you were Not-My-People, I say to you, You-Are-My-People."

That is how Peter saw us, like Gomer, the forgiven wife. Who better than Peter knew the forgiveness of the Lord? So he described us, the church, this way: "You are a chosen race, a royal priesthood, . . . God's own people. . . . Once you were no people but now you are God's people; once you had not received mercy, but now you have received mercy" (1 Pet. 2:9-10). So, yes, we are Gomer, the grateful recipient of God's love.

But we are more than Gomer, more than the world God so loved; we are more than the recipient of grace's pardon. We are also Hosea! We are the *giver* of the love with which God so loves the world. We, by the power of God's grace, exhibit in our daily lives the *hesed,* the steadfast love of God. We are the body of Christ who exemplify in the character of our common life (as husband and wife, mother, father, sister and brother and friend) the faithful loving-kindness of God, the stubborn, patient, costly love of God.

Yes, we are Gomer, how can we forget, forgiven sinners all, recipients of the grace of God's pardon. And yet, we are also, by the grace of God's power, Hosea. We are the husband who will not discard the wife, we are the friend who stays a friend through the ups and downs that all close friendships have, we are brothers and sisters in Christ who do not live by the fickle affections of this world, but by the rule of God's love, God's costly, steadfast, never giving up, suffering love. That is our holy calling: to practice that kind of love in our human relationships, so that the world may look at us and have hope.

In the 1960s Joni Mitchell sang a song about people searching "for love that sticks around." By God's grace, we, Gomer, have found the "love that sticks around." By God's grace, we, Hosea, are able to live it.

Notes

1. Frederick Buechner, *Peculiar Treasures* (New York: Harper & Row, 1979), p. 43.
2. The phrase of Martin Buber, *The Prophetic Faith* (New York: Harper & Row, 1949), p. 119.

10
Jonah

The Book of Jonah may be the most entertaining book in the Bible. Nowhere is the humor of God more evident than in this little book about a prophet named Jonah. Jonah was the first foreign missionary in the Bible—the first and the worst. The story is based on the worst preacher in the Bible, but one through whom God worked out His purpose. Therefore the story becomes a parable of the sovereignty of God: of His freedom to act as He sees fit and of His power to use even a scoundrel like Jonah for His purpose. Listen to God's comedy called *Jonah*.

Act 1

"Arise, go to Nineveh" was God's first word to Jonah. "Go to Nineveh and preach my judgment. Tell them I know of their wickedness" (see 1:1-2).

Jonah was dumbfounded. "Nineveh? Me, preach your word there? Nineveh: that bunch of cruel no-account sinners! Don't cast your pearls before swine. Not Nineveh. *No way, Yahweh!"*

Nineveh—the capital of Assyria. To the Hebrew people the name represented the worst of moral and political evil. The very name brought fear and disgust to the Hebrew heart. Assyria was a cruel, ruthless world power.

God Almighty should have no business with Nineveh. Jonah was like many of God's people. He drew a circle around God's love. God Almighty has to do with justice and mercy: He judges others and shows mercy to me!

Nineveh is the capital city of the enemy, and through the years we have just changed the names: from Nineveh to Babylon, to Rome, to Berlin, to Moscow, Havana, and Iran. Nineveh is the land where godless people live and threaten to take us over. My God! They don't need sermons; they just need judgment.

And Nineveh is the shadowy land of our prejudice. Our fear draws circles around God's love and excludes those who are different. We hate in others what we fear in ourselves, so most anytime, anyplace we might meet a Ninevite.

We each have our Ninevehs, those places and peoples outside the circle. Many different things cause us to draw closed the circle. Race draws some; politics draw others. Our psychological makeup draws others. Regretfully, even education erects Ninevehs. We have been taught to seek the best knowledge we can find by our families, so we go to the best schools and find ourselves cut off from our families. As pastors have gotten more education and churches more affluent, we have cut ourselves off not only from the poor but also from blue-collar people. Instead of widening the circle, our education has tightened it.

So we've drawn circles around God's love and called God in to police the boundaries. How startling then to hear "Jonah, arise and go to Nineveh."

When Jonah heard the command he replied, "Who are you kidding, Lord? No self-respecting Jew would set foot in Nineveh, nor any self-respecting God, I might add."

In short, Jonah said no. To be sure, the idea had to scare him, but it seems to me that the reason that he refused was that he had the sneaky feeling that God might work some mercy there and God's mercy didn't belong in Nineveh. So he fled, not so much in fear of Nineveh's evil but in fear that God might save that sorry city. Nineveh needed to pay for its sins, and Jonah wanted no part of a mission that might lead to repentance.

Act 2

So Jonah took a ship to Tarshish. God said, "Jonah, go east." Jonah went west. God said, "Head toward Assyria"; Jonah took a trip toward Spain.

While the ship was on its way west a storm arose. Jonah was asleep downstairs, and the scared sailors woke him up and dragged him upstairs. They asked him to pray to his God to still the storm. When prayer didn't work they resorted to magic. They tossed dice to see who was responsible. The dice fell to poor, hapless Jonah. "OK, Buster, what's your story?" "Well, I'm a Hebrew," he said. "I worship Yahweh, who controls the land and the sea (not to speak of these dice). It's all my fault. Throw me overboard." We don't know whether this was an act of gallantry—an attempt to save the sailors' lives—or of despair—a desire to die rather than live in a world where God would try to save Nineveh! But we suspect the latter.

Overboard went Jonah. The sea calmed down and the sailors were so impressed that they took up an offering and decided to serve Yahweh—which was not the last time a church has tossed somebody overboard and called it religion!

Act 3

Here comes the part about the big fish. This section has been subjected to some of the most foolish scrutiny of any part of the Bible. We get so hung up about what happened inside the fish that we ignore what was going on inside of Jonah.

In his novel *Moby Dick,* Herman Melville satirized the rationalizing attempts to explain how Jonah could have lived three days inside the whale's belly. Some argued that Jonah hid in the hollow tooth of the whale for three days; others that Jonah hid in a dead whale for the three days; others argued that he was found by a ship named *The Whale.*

All explanations miss the whole point. If it was important to God to give us the details, He would have. If we concentrate on the chemical composition of the whale's digestive juices, then we'll miss the whole drama of what was going on between God and Jonah. Jonah, who could not believe that God would love the Ninevites, would die rather than serve this kind of God. And God, who loved both Nineveh and Jonah, would not let Jonah so easily consign himself to damnation and death.

As Jonah was tossed overboard and slowly descended into the depths of the ocean, God sent a great fish (species unknown) to rescue Jonah. The fish caught Jonah's descent and carried him from the netherland of the deep back to life on shore. Even Jonah's final attempt at death did not separate him from God's presence and purpose. It was a demonstration of God's saving mercy.

Act 4

Three days later the fish spat Jonah onto dry land. Jonah was no better after the ride than before it. The whale changed Jonah's *destination* but not his *disposition*. It changed Jonah's *geography* but not his *theology*. Jonah still thought God was crazy. Anyone who thinks that Jonah now was a properly chastened and repentent preacher is badly mistaken. God called him again there and then on the beach. This time Jonah went, not happily but grudgingly, not because he was filled with love for Nineveh but because once you've tried to escape in a ship, been tossed overboard, and been carried back to shore in a fish's belly, you figure that you don't have a whale of a choice left!

Jonah stalked to Nineveh, sullen and angry but determined to go preach God's message of judgment. Maybe God would destroy them after all. He'd like to see the fireworks anyway.

So he went through the streets and preached hellfire and damnation.

His sermon had three points: 1) God is just; 2) You are sinners; 3) Bye-Bye. He gave no hymn of invitation, left town, and sat down outside on a hill, waiting, hoping, for the blood to spurt, the walls to burn, and screams to pierce the air.

Act 5

What happened? Much to his dismay, the city *repented*—from the king all the way down to the commoners. The crooning of Yahweh's Caruso must have worked! His words struck their hearts and brought repentance—even though they were spoken through the mouth of a bad-spirited scoundrel of a prophet. God is powerful enough to work through men and women with bad theology, mixed motives, hard hearts, flawed politics, and messed-up grammar. As badly as we preach, as badly as we live, God will somehow use us. It is our only hope as preachers; it is our only hope as witnesses; it is our only hope as the church—that God can use us Jonahs, mean-spirited and misguided as we often are. God's treasure indeed is in earthen vessels; but still God's power is revealed.

Nineveh repented, and the king's speech of repentance is a beautiful model of true reverence.

"*Who knows*, God may yet repent and turn from his fierce anger, so we perish not" (see 3:9).

"Who knows": the words of one who reverences the Holy otherness of God. No deal making with the Almighty. No attempt to manipulate Him by magic. Not "OK, God, if you save us, we'll repent." "Who knows. . . ."

That is a deeper reverence than we often practice. We think we've got God all figured out. We've reduced God to some principle, some theological idea. We can predict what He is going to do. There's a smugness to our faith. The pagan king of Nineveh had more reverence. "Who knows, God may yet. . . ."

There are times when all our knowledge becomes an idol and we need to stop talking about God and stop telling God all we know about Him and, with sackcloth and ashes, with humble minds and hearts, say, "Who knows. . . ."

The Scripture then records some amazing words: "When God saw what they did, how they turned from their evil way, God repented of the evil which he had said he would do to them" (v. 10).

God changed His mind because they changed their hearts. He repented because they repented.

That boggles our minds. The God who created the universe, who set the stars in space and designed the orbits for the planets, this same God is affected by me. Our actions make a difference—they make a difference in this world, and they make a difference to God.

Away with the Greek god fashioned by the philosophers made distant, apathetic, unchangeable—the unmoved mover.

The biblical God is the God of Abraham and Sarah, Moses and Jesus, and us. This God is not aloof, unmoved. He is there with the slaves in a fight for freedom, with women in childbirth, in a hospital room, in the arms of a mother starving to death, in the pew, in the ballot box, in the trustees' meeting, on the gallows, on a cross.

What goes on with you makes a difference. It matters what you do. God is at work in every decision, every deed, every moment, working with us toward the redemption of this world. God is not just a principle of justice, good, or love. He is no unmoved mover, no cosmic watchmaker. He is our Father, righteous and merciful.

This God changed His mind because Nineveh's people changed their hearts.

Act 6

What a nice turn in the story; but, oh, was Jonah angry! Now he had egg on his face. God told him to preach doom, and God then had spared them. That made Jonah a false prophet. The Old Testament is clear—that's how you tell a true prophet from a false one—whether their words come true. That made Jonah a false prophet.

Not only had God saved that ungodly people; He had made a liar out of Jonah.

Jonah flew into a rage. He quoted Scripture at God—a familiar tactic we all use when we get mad at God.

I knew you would do it! I knew—and I quote—"that thou art a gracious God and merciful, slow to anger, and abounding in steadfast love, and repentest of evil" (4:2)—end quote Exodus 34:6. I remember that verse. I did memory work as a Junior. You're soft on sin. I knew you wouldn't do anything. That's why I didn't want to go. You say you are just—prove it! Your mercy looks like softness to me, or impotence.

Listen, Almighty God who preaches judgment and practices mercy, I would rather die than live in a world with a God like you, so let me die.

Jonah stomped angrily off, wanting judgment, not mercy, wanting justice, not God. And here we stand with Jonah saying,

> I hate God's enemies
> with perfect hatred.
> Why can't God
> do as much?[1]

Jonah stomped away and sat down, and a beautiful plant grew over him to become a green leafy shade. Jonah rejoiced in this simple sign of goodness. Something was alive and good. It was an emotional, cathartic time for Jonah—as when we see the first green bud of spring or see a rainbow after a storm. But, as dawn came, a worm crept to the plant and chewed it to pieces. The plant died and Jonah was furious. The sun beat down its heat and Jonah was cross-eyed with rage.

God said, "Jonah, are you right to be angry about the plant's death?"

Jonah said, "Am I right to be angry—Am I right? I'm so angry I could just curl up and die. Here you go and save 120,000 of the most evil people in your sickeningly sweet world and then turn around and let this little plant die. Am I mad?"

God replied, "Jonah, you pity a little plant which you did not create or tend or grow, and which perished in the night. Can I not feel pity for a town of 120,000 people who cannot even tell their right hands from their left hands, not to mention the animals?" (see 4:9-11).

Conclusion

That is how the story ends. It ends with the surprise of God's mercy, and we have the same choice as Jonah—to sit and sulk at God's goodness or to find joy in His mercy.

His word to us is the same as to Jonah. What's more important: your theology or these people, your principles or these people, your reputation or these people? Isn't it even better that I, God, should change my mind and risk my reputation than that these people should die?

It was the same message He made through Jesus, who gave mercy to sinners and ate with prostitutes and tax-collectors, who told parables about prodigals and said that the final word is the surprise of God's grace.

So what do you want—principles or God; what you deserve or what God gives? What do you want to stake your life on: what you can accomplish or God's mercy, God's free, unexpected mercy?

Note

1. Thomas John Carlisle, *You! Jonah* (Grand Rapids: William B. Eerdmans, 1968), p. 43.

11
Daniel

The story of Daniel is "an epic of moral courage."[1] It has shaped many of us in our early years. It depicts the courage to say no and to stand up for what you believe. I remember from my youth more than one sermon on Daniel and the hymn that often went with it: "Dare to Be Brave; Dare to Be True."

The Book of Daniel is the source. The first six chapters of the book are set in Babylon and tell of Daniel and his three friends Shadrach, Meshach, and Abednego. It is the sixth century BC and their story is the story of many Jews carried off into Babylonian captivity after Babylonia had ransacked Jerusalem. Their plight was the plight of many Jews: "How can we sing the Lord's song in a strange land?" How can we stay faithful in a land of another religion and another set of values? We can learn from these first six chapters. America is not nearly as Christian as we once believed. The dominant cultural pattern is becoming increasingly pagan, I fear. How do we sing the Lord's song in a strange land?

The last six chapters of Daniel reflect the final setting of the book. It is second century Judah, and the Jews are suffering under the tyranny of an evil, foreign king, Antiochus Epiphanes. The visions of Daniel in the first six chapters are, in the last six chapters, extended and applied under the guidance of the Spirit of God. It was and is a book for times of crisis. It speaks of faith and wisdom and courage.

The story begins with Daniel as a young man. Even as a teenager he had the courage to say no (chap. 1).

Daniel's early years were lived amid the stormy days of the fall of Jerusalem. King Nebuchadnezzar took the city by force. Then he gave instructions to select a number of the most promising young men and bring them to Babylon, where they would be given the best education possible and prepared for government service. Daniel was one of those picked for his physical and intellectual promise. Like a young Rhodes Scholar on his way to Oxford, Daniel was brought to Babylon. (Well, not quite like a Rhodes Scholar; Rhodes Scholars have a chance to turn it down!)

He went with three friends: Hananiah, Mishael, and Azariah. When they arrived the first thing the Babylonians did was to give them new names. Daniel was called Belteshazzar, Hananiah was called Shadrach, Mishael was called Meshach, and Azariah was called Abednego.

Note that they accepted their new Babylonian names. They did not say no to everything. If courage is the strength to say no, wisdom is the ability of knowing when to say yes and when to say no. To say no to everything is not courage; it is muleheadedness. It is not moral integrity; it is priggishness. There is no virtue in saying no to everything. But an even greater danger is the tyranny of having to say yes to everything. The word no keeps you free. Practice it daily. *No.* Wisdom is the knowledge of when to say no. Courage is the strength to say it.

You see, not everything the world has to offer is bad. Daniel accepted Babylonian education and a Babylonian name. But he knew when to say no and he said it. That was one part wisdom, one part courage.

Daniel knew where to draw the line, and he drew it at the point of diet. As a regular part of the three-year training program the young men were fed from the royal table. The first time Daniel looked at the table he knew a choice had to be made. There on the table was pork, meat forbidden by Jewish law; there was food prepared in a nonkosher way; there was food which had first been sacrificed to idols; and there was wine which, while not forbidden by Jewish law, was accompanied with warning about its dangers.

Daniel could accept a Babylonian name, but he could not accept a Babylonian diet. He knew when to say no. He could have argued: it is not what goes into your body that matters but what comes out of the heart that matters! He could have said, I'll go along until my education is finished; when in Babylon do as the Babylonians do; afterward I'll follow my Jewish tradition. He could have said, "Oh, I'll never see Jerusalem again; so what's the difference!"

But Daniel had the courage to say no. You might argue, "Such a little thing is the dietary regulation. Why risk it all for that! Why not wait for the really big tests of faith." But it is the little tests of life that prepare you for the big ones. "He who is faithful in a very little is faithful also in much" (Luke 16:10), Jesus said. Woe unto the one who waits for a life and death decision in order to stand for his faith. By then he has given it away bit by bit.

So Daniel said no. He made a deal with the king's servant: "You let us take a vegetable and water diet for ten days. Then compare our appearance with the other youth who eat at the king's table." At the end of the ten days Daniel and his friends looked healthier than the rest, so they were able to stay on their Jewish diet.

The story says that God blessed Daniel and his three friends. They grew strong and wise. Daniel stood for his faith. He had the wisdom to know when to say no and the courage to stick to it.

From that time on Daniel became a rising star in the king's court. In chapter 2 he interpreted King Nebuchadnezzar's dream. Like the young Joseph in Egypt, young Daniel demonstrated the superiority of God's wisdom over all the other wisdom of the world. The king was so grateful that he promoted Daniel and his three friends to high positions of leadership.

This brings us to chapter 3 in this epic of moral courage. Now Shadrach, Meshach, and Abednego take center stage.

Nebuchadnezzar had erected a giant gold idol and made the decree: All shall bow down to this image; if not, they shall be cast into a fiery furnace! Some Chaldeans went to the king and made this accusation: O Great King, you have made your decree. But there are three Jews whom you promoted to leadership positions, Shadrach, Meshach, and Abednego, who are not obeying you and who refuse to bow down to the golden image which you set up.

King Nebuchadnezzar flew into a furious rage and demanded that they be brought before him. "Is it true that you will not worship the golden image? If you are now ready to go ahead and bow down to it, I'll let bygones be bygones; but if you refuse, into the fiery furnace you will go. Who will deliver you then?" (see vv. 14-15).

In one of the great moments of faith in the Bible they replied to the king:

"If it be so, our God whom we serve is able to deliver us from the burning fiery furnace; and he will deliver us out of your hand, O king. *But if not,* be it known to you, O king, that we will not serve your gods or worship the golden image" (see Dan. 3:17-18).

Immortal words of faith: *but if not.* My God will rescue me; *but if not* I shall still believe. That is real faith. You go to the doctor and the doctor has bad news. You pray, "Lord, help me survive this disease; *but if not,* no matter what, you are still my God." You do what is right, but nothing in life seems to be going the way it should. You pray, "Lord, help me; help me save my job, or my marriage; *but if not,* still will I serve thee." You find out that being a Christian does *not* pay and that good guys sometimes finish last. You say, "Lord, no matter the results, I will not give up on living as I think a Christian should."

That is *real* faith. The cheap religion of our day says, "Believe and all shall be yours!" This sales pitch goes: "Have faith and God will reward you." What a shallow, selfish faith that is. Shadrach, Meshach, and Abednego would never make it as guests on some religious TV shows. They had a kind of faith Jesus would exemplify years later.

Remember in the garden of Gethsemane? "Father, if thou be willing, remove this cup from me; *nevertheless* not my will, but thine, be done" (Luke 22:42). Like the faith of those three men in the Book of Daniel: "Our God can deliver us—*but if not* still we shall not bow down to your idol." It is curious how unassuming the grammar of faith is—those commonplace words and phrases, those almost overlooked conjunctions. *But if not. Nevertheless.* But they are the words which make up faith. Give us the faith to say, *but if not, nevertheless, no matter what, still* I shall believe. Faith is not some magic amount of belief that will ensure a miracle. Jesus said all you need is a mustard-seed size of faith to move mountains. Faith is the determination to trust in God and stay faithful to Him no matter what happens.

For these three young men their faith ended in a miracle. It does not always. Faith that *requires* a miracle is no faith at all. But thanks be to God, sometimes faith does end in miracles. And it did here.

The king had them bound and thrown into the fiery furnace. As King Nebuchadnezzar looked into the furnace he rubbed his eyes; he couldn't believe what he saw. "Did not we cast three men bound into the fire?" "True, O king," his soldiers said. "But I see *four* men loose, walking in the fire, and they are not hurt and the appearance of the fourth one is like a son of the gods" (3:24-25).

Then the king opened the door and out the three came, Shadrach, Meshach, and Abednego, unharmed—not a hair on their head singed. You couldn't even smell smoke on their clothes.

The king said, "Blessed be the God of Shadrach, Meshach, and Abednego who has sent his angel and delivered [them]" (v. 28). And we echo his praise. Blessed be our God! And then we add, And blessed are those who have the faith to say, "*But if not,* I shall still serve my God!"

The next way Daniel's courage was demonstrated was by his faithfulness in the interpretation of dreams. It takes courage to speak God's word even when you know the results might not be pleasant. Daniel had the courage to speak forth what God had to say.

One night Daniel got a call in the middle of the night. King Nebuchadnezzar wanted him *then* and *there.* Daniel pulled his trousers on over his pajama bottoms, slipped on his overcoat, and went.

The king was in a cold sweat. He had had a nightmare. All of his magicians and astrologers had tried, with no luck, to interpret the dream. That's why Daniel was summoned.

Stammering and stuttering, the king reported the nightmare: there was this enormous tree so heavy with leaves and fruit that

Daniel

it gave shade all over the world and birds and beasts flocked there for shelter and food.

That's you, O king, you and your kingdom, Daniel interpreted.

Then the king went on: a watcher, a holy one from heaven, came down and gave orders that the tree was to be chopped down, its branches cut off and all its leaves and fruit scattered.

That decree comes from the Most High, said Daniel.

The king went on: The stump of the tree had its heart changed from a man's heart to a beast's heart. The beast now ate grass with the oxen and got wet with the dew of heaven; his hair grew long and matted and his nails long like a bird's.

That's what is in store for you, Daniel said. I wish it were not so, but that is what it means. "That's to help you get back in touch with reality.... You've gotten so used to being treated like a God, you've started believing you are one."[2]

Daniel laid it out for the king to ponder. Here's your choice, King Nebuchadnezzar: When it happens, if you come to your senses and realize that God is God and you are not, if you repent and decide to be a king who reveres God and does *justice*, who practices righteousness and shows mercy to the weak, then your kingdom will be given back. If not, I hope you develop the taste for grass because that's going to be breakfast, lunch, and supper for you.

And so it happened. Nebuchadnezzar took an unexpected leave of absence to wander around on all fours. Then one day he looked up at the heavens and got back his right mind. His beast's heart was changed back into a man's heart, the kind of heart that knew to praise God. Leaving all fours to walk like a man again, he cried out, "O Most High God, your kingdom is forever and ever" (see 4:34).

Sure enough. Not only did he get his mind back but also his throne, all because Daniel was brave enough to interpret the dream as God intended—to teach the king a lesson in reality.

One more scene. One final act of courage. Now Daniel is older. He has established himself with the third successive king, Darius.

Darius has reorganized the empire and decided to make Daniel one of its highest officials. Predictably, the evil eye of envy took hold of some of the other bureaucrats. They schemed to topple Daniel.

First they tried to find something in his life that they could use as blackmail. But after hiring the best private eyes in the business they could uncover nothing. "He was," as the Scriptures record, "faithful, neither was there any error or fault found in him" (6:4, KJV).

The envy-driven plotters now devised a scheme to trap Daniel. They used Daniel's loyalty to God as bait.

They persuaded Darius to issue a decree that upon the pain of being thrown to the lions, no inhabitant of Babylon was to pray for thirty days to any god but Darius. Darius liked the sound of it. Not realizing that it was a trick to trap Daniel, whom he admired, Darius signed the decree.

Daniel again had a choice to make. Every day he would open his windows which faced Jerusalem and pray to his God. He knew now that if he continued to do this he would find himself thrown like Meow Mix to some hungry lions. He could have prayed secretly, not opened the windows, and escaped punishment. He knew he could have kept practicing his faith in private with no harm. But a faith that is only a private faith and not also a public faith is no faith at all. So knowing full well the consequences, Daniel flung open the windows, prayed his prayer, and found himself eyeball to eyeball with some ornery lions.

The heart-torn Darius, knowing that he had been tricked but unwilling to break his own decree, led Daniel to the lions' den. He said to Daniel, "May your God whom you serve continually deliver you!" (v. 16).

The king hardly slept at all that night. The next morning he rushed down to the lions' den and cried out, "Daniel, did your God deliver you?" He opened the doors and there was Daniel playing with the lions like a bunch of kittens. Daniel looked up and said, "My God sent an angel and shut their mouths" (see vv. 21-22).

The old joke has some truth to it: the lions weren't able to eat Daniel because he was all backbone.

We don't know much about the rest of Daniel's life. We know that he not only interpreted dreams for others but also had some visions of his own. Like his great successor on the Isle of Patmos, John, the writer of Revelation, Daniel saw visions of the final triumph of God. These visions are the stuff that make for courage. His visions picture the great, good news: God's kingdom will reign forever and ever. God is greater than Babylon or Rome. He is greater than Pharaoh, Nebuchadnezzar, Darius, Antiochus, or Caesar. The good shall finally be rewarded and the wicked shall reap their just deserts. Regardless of how it appears at times, God and His good shall prevail.

That vision gives us courage. It helps us remain strong in the face of temptation. It helps us take heart and persevere during dark times of adversity. It was this kind of courage-making vision Jesus had in mind when He said,

"In the world you have tribulation, but take courage; I have overcome the world" (John 16:33, NASB).

Notes

1. Clarence E. Macartney, *Sermons on Old Testament Heroes* (Nashville: Abingdon Press, 1935), p. 34.
2. Frederick Buechner, *Peculiar Treasures* (New York: Harper & Row, 1979), p. 21. This whole dream sequence follows Buechner's delightful rendition of the scene.

12
Job

The story of Job concerns the deepest of questions: the problem of suffering in a world created by a loving God. It wrestles with the challenge raised by MacLeish's words in his play on Job, *J. B.*:

> If God is God He is not good,
> If God is good He is not God.[1]

How do we answer the problem of the suffering of the innocent, of bad things happening to good people in a world created by a good God? MacLeish's Nickles suggests to us: either God is powerful and not loving, or He is loving and not powerful. Such are the deeps the story of Job seeks to traverse.

Job is Everyman. Job is the good man gone bankrupt because he is swindled. Job is the mother holding her dead child. Job is the man whose wife commits suicide. Job is the Jew watching the newsreels of six million other Jews being exterminated by a so-called "Christian" regime. Job's story at some point in life becomes my story and yours.

Job is a book that wrestles with human anguish. It denounces pat answers because pat answers are what we often get instead of love, because pat answers are what we often seek instead of God. Listen now to the story of Job.

Once, many years ago, lived a man named Job. You could have searched the world over and not found a better man. The Bible

108

says that he was "blameless and upright, one who feared God and turned away from evil" (1:1). He had it all. He was the epitome of a good and successful man. He had seven sons and three daughters and more sheep, camels, oxen, and donkeys than you could count. The Midrash, that Jewish commentary on Scripture, goes on to add that everything he had acquired he had acquired honestly; his house was open on all four sides so that every beggar through town could sit down and eat; he helped the sick, the widows, the orphans, all who had need.[2]

Then it happened—a series of calamities, awesome in their extent and their suddenness. A messenger came running in and said, "The Sabeans took your donkeys and killed your servants watching them." Then before he had even finished another came and said, "Lightning struck your sheep barn, burned the whole flock—even the shepherds were killed." Then, as he was finishing, another servant rushed in and cried, "The Chaldeans raided your camels, killed your camel drivers. I am the only one left." And while he was still speaking, another messenger came and said, "Sir, your sons and daughters were at a party. A great windstorm came and flattened the house, and they were all killed." (See 1:13-19.) In one day Job had lost all his children and all his fortune. But Job refused to curse God.

Then he himself came down with leprosy. Sores covered his whole body, from head to foot, and he went, sat on an ash heap, and scraped his boils with a piece of broken pottery. His wife urged him to curse God and die, but Job refused.

The book pictures Satan licking his lips in anticipation of what Job will surely do—curse God. Satan challenged God: so you think Job is a good and faithful man, do you? Anybody can be so in good times. Let's see what he does in bad times.

So one of the key themes of the book is stated nine verses into the book: "Will Job serve God for nothing?" Do any of us serve God with no thought of return? To this point in the story, even through all his calamities Job had been a model of righteousness and faithfulness.

Then came Job's so-called friends, Eliphaz, Bildad, and Zophar. When they saw him they could not believe their eyes. They could hardly recognize him. When they saw what had happened they broke down and wept. They were models of good pastoral care: for seven days they did not open their mouths. They grieved with Job. They were just there in sympathetic, compassionate presence. A Midrash says that in deference to the mourner one imitates his behavior. When Job arose they arose, when he ate they ate, when he drank they drank, when he wept they wept. We are moved by their compassion and good sense. They must have had at least two units of clinical pastoral education.

But then after seven days they opened their mouths, and when they did they turned to fools. Job began to question the conventional religion of his day which said that life was easy to explain: good things happen to good people; bad things happen to bad people; God rewards the just and punishes the wicked. Simple. But Job questioned it, and, as he did, his friends chose to defend it.

First, Job cried out in grief's anger: "I wish I had never been born. I wish I had died at birth. I wish I could die now." (See chap. 3.)

His friends were scandalized by his anger and brazenness, and they began to speak.

Eliphaz first had his say: "Job, you should not be so impatient. God is faithful and just. He will work things out. Just have faith. You comforted others in grief; now take your own advice. If you are innocent, brother Job, you have nothing to worry about. In God's plan good guys always win, so hang in there, Job. I'm telling you this for your own good. Be patient." (See chaps. 4—5.)

Then Bildad spoke: "God doesn't make mistakes, Job. You reap what you sow. Your dead children must have been guilty of something. Now what you need to do is to get right with God. Just look at history: those who forget God wither and die. Don't you know, brother Job, that good things happen to good people and bad things happen to bad people? So don't look at *God* for the answer; go look in the mirror."

Next Zophar entered the conversation. He said, "Job, you are obviously guilty; God is punishing you *less* than you deserve and you just add to it by your complaints. Don't you know: God's ways are beyond our comprehension. He is Mystery. Do not presume or demand to understand it all. (Good enough theology but wrong time and place.) Get your heart right and God will bless you." (See chap. 11.)

With three friends like these, the saying goes, who needs enemies! Job called them "worthless physicians" and added, "If you would be silent that would be your wisdom" (see 16:1-3). Paul Scherer says, "When you meet trouble with a truism you make trouble." Not all they believed was false and some of it true, but they were fools to say it so glibly in the face of *another's* tragedy.

Then Job defended himself: "You do not understand the depth of my grief. My burden is as heavy as all the sand of the sea to me." (See 6:1ff.) You say, Be patient? How can I be patient? Am I made of stone or bronze? Cannot I have feelings?" (See 6:11-12.)

Then Job turned to God and challenged God: "You are responsible for my pain, but it makes no sense to me. I do *not* deserve what I have received. You use me for target practice, you laugh at my misery. You are like a tyrant, a wild beast, a ruthless warrior. I am torn apart by my grief, destroyed by disease" (see vv. 13-17). Job's scream filled the air: "Earth, do not absorb my blood; let the cry of it wander all over the earth" (see 16:18). All Job had left was words, and he knew how to use them. As Wiesel says, "He made them quiver; he made them scream."[3] "Earth, [do not absorb] my blood!"

Upon hearing Job's words, the three friends attacked him even more ferociously—all in the name of religion.

Eliphaz told Job: "Job, you have just forgotten all those sins you have committed. Surely, you robbed the clothes off the backs of brothers. You must have refused food to beggars. You must have sent widows and orphans away with nothing. Does not God see everything? Search your heart, Job. Be honest. Job, make peace with God. Stop making him your enemy." (See 22:1-28.) Then Eliphaz threw in a dagger: "God brings down the proud and saves the humble" (22:29).

Job, grown weary of his friends, refused to debate their arguments and instead talked about God with new poignance:

"[Once God and I were as close as could be. There was a time] when his lamp shone up on my head, and by his light I walked through darkness" (29:3). "There was a time when the friendship of God was upon my tent [when God was close, when friends were everywhere, when my children were around my side]" (29:4-6).

"But now my wealth is gone, my friends are gone, my children are gone, even God is gone. I look for him in the front, in the back, to the right and to the left, but God is nowhere to be found" (see 23:8-9).

And while earlier Job would close his speeches with a prayer to God, now he could not even pray. What he did next was raise his last defense. He had prayed for someone to come plead his case and defend him—a mediator, an advocate, a redeemer—but none came. So now he became his own defense attorney.

He listed one by one all the ways a person could sin and at each point said, "I am innocent." Then he closed his argument, put his signature on his legal brief, and said, "I rest my case; now, God, your turn to answer me" (see 31:35). And the last verse of chapter 31 says, "The words of Job are ended" (v. 40).

Then a new speaker arrived, a brash and bright young theologian named Elihu. He had been overhearing the debate, dying to break in. He said, "All of you are wrong, but I, while young, have God's Spirit in me, so I can bring wisdom to this discussion. My words are like wine in new wineskins with no vent; I must speak before I burst" (see 32:19-20). Sounds like a seminarian.

Elihu debated all that had been said and then concluded: "I have yet something to say on God's behalf. [Let a man lose himself in adoration of God and he will have no room for self-pity. Be assured, Job, God strengthens and purifies you through adversity]" (36:1-14). "He delivers the afflicted by their affliction, and opens their ear by adversity" (36:15). At that moment I am sure Job wished his ears were shut—along with Elihu's mouth. Then Elihu closed his argument with a glorious description of God's grandeur and tied a bow on his speech with the final innuendo directed at Job. "[You must remember, Job, that God] 'does not regard any who are wise in their own conceit' " (37:24)—an unwitting self-condemnation—Elihu the pot calling the kettle black.

Then, as Elihu finished his speech, God could no longer be kept silent. If He could not be roused by Job's anger, He was by Elihu's smug theologizing. He answered Job from out of a whirlwind. Job asked for God to answer him, and answer him God did.

But the answer was in the form of a series of questions, outrageous, impossible rhetorical questions:

"*Where were you when I laid the foundation of the earth? . . . Who [measured the earth and] laid its cornerstone? . . . Have you entered into the springs of the sea or walked in the recesses of the deep? . . . Where is the way to the dwelling place of light? Have you entered into the storehouses of the snow? Has the rain a father? Can you bind the [stars]? Who has put wisdom in the clouds?*" (38:5-6, 16, 19, 22, 28, 31, 36). And God was just getting warmed up. *"Is the wild ox willing to serve you? Do you give the horse his might? Is it by your wisdom that the hawk soars? Is it by your command that the eagle mounts up?"* (see 39:9, 19, 26-27).

Then God concluded, "*Shall a faultfinder contend with the Almighty?[Now you answer me!]*" (see 40:2).

Then Job said, "I am of small account; . . . [I shut my mouth.] I will proceed no further" (40:4-5).

But God kept on. "[Stand up like a man and answer my questions.] *Have you an arm like God and can you thunder with a voice like his?[Would you like to play God for a while? Come take my place, if you wish]*" (see 40:7, 9).

Then God took off on a series of questions about two mysterious monsters—Behemoth and Leviathan. *"Can you corral these two* forces? Can you catch the sea monster with a fish hook? Can you lasso a dinosaur? Can you control all the awesome and mysterious forces of light and forces of darkness?" (see 40:15 to 41:34).

"Then Job answered: 'I talked about things I did not understand, things too wonderful and too terrible for me which I could not understand. I have heard all my life about your glory and splendor and majesty and now this moment my eyes see thee. So I repent in dust and ashes'" (see 42:5-6).

God, however, did not let Job languish in self-despising. He picked him up and dusted him off. But first God spoke to the four friends and said, "I am angry with you because you have spoken falsehood about me. Your answers were more false than Job's questions." (See 42:7-9.)

Then God blessed Job with new children, seven more sons and three more daughters, with new health and new wealth. And Job lived until 140, long enough to be a grandfather and great-grandfather and great-great-grandfather.

There are some people who do not like the happy ending. Some think it is out of place. Some like Job better before he repented than after. Elie Wiesel says, "He should not have given in so easily. He should have continued to protest, to refuse the handouts."[4]

But Job had seen and heard enough. He did not get his children back, but he got ten more, not to replace them, not to erase his grief, but to give him new blessings and new days of joy.

And he never got direct answers to his questions, but he got the answer of the presence of God, and that, after all, is what we most need in times of crisis—not answers, but God. It is the experience of God's presence that lets us live in the mystery of God's justice and mercy, of His love and power, in the mix of life's pleasure and pain.

Job wanted answers, but more than answers he wanted God; and God Himself was what Job got an earful and eyeful of that day from out of the whirlwind.

We who live "in Christ" read this story through the lenses of the Christ event and see even more in its longing and pathos.

Job asked for a mediator (9:33), an advocate (16:19), a redeemer (19:25), someone to plead his case, to stand by him and with him and for him. He knew not for whom he asked, but we do:

One who would come from heaven and take on our flesh, who would walk our paths. One who would bear our sorrows and our griefs. One who would love us and give himself for us. One who would conquer the grave and ascend to the right hand of the Father. One who would give us hope in eternal life, in a final justice and final love. One who would promise us a place of glad, heavenly reunion.

A voice from a whirlwind was all Job got then, but God would later answer his deepest longing beyond his wildest expectations.

He would send us His Son who would be a Redeemer, a Mediator, a High Priest in heaven who has walked this earth.

Hebrews 4:15 says: "We have not a high priest who is unable to sympathize with our weaknesses, but one who in every respect has been tempted as we are, yet without sin," one who has felt the sting of abandonment but who still prayed, "*My* God, *My* God, why hast thou forsaken me."

The writer of Hebrews also says, "Let us come boldly unto the throne of grace that we may obtain mercy, and find grace to help in the time of need" (v. 16, KJV).

Almighty God, We come before you broken of body, with aching heart. Take our heartbreak, our questions, our complaints, and forge them by your presence into a grace to sustain us, the grace of the Lord Jesus Christ in whose name we come boldly before you, Amen.

Notes

1. Archibald MacLeish, *J. B.* (Cambridge: The Riverside Press, 1958), p. 14.
2. Elie Wiesel, *Messengers of God* (New York: Random House, 1976), pp. 215-16.
3. Ibid., p. 229.
4. Ibid., p. 234.

13
Ruth

Who was this young Moabite woman named Ruth? She has enchanted Dante, Milton, and Bunyan. The Book of Ruth itself is a work of art, a cameo set in the Old Testament. No less than Goethe called the book the most beautiful "little whole" in the Old Testament.

The modern Jew still hears the story today in its entirety every year at the Festival of Shabuoth. Unfortunately, Ruth is virtually ignored in the Christian church. In a major lectionary of the church it is left entirely out.[1]

We are much the poorer for having ignored it. It is a gorgeous story with deep spiritual insight. It is the story of *hesed,* that Hebrew word which is closest to what in the New Testament we call *grace*. *Hesed*—the word that combines kindness and loyalty—is often translated "loving-kindness." *Hesed* may be the most important description of God in the Old Testament.

What startles us about this story is that *hesed* is not dramatically introduced by God from heaven. *Hesed* happens between people and was set in motion by a young Moabite woman named Ruth. What is startling about this story is its very ordinariness. God was at work not among the heroic patriarchs, not in the political capitals, not amid visions, dreams, and miracles, but, rather, in the commonplace of life, in a country town called Bethlehem, and in the midst of ordinary people like you and me who work and eat and love.

God stays in the shadows. His *hesed* is worked out through the extraordinary kindness ordinary people show to one another.

Ruth demonstrates the *"contagion of kindness."* She lives *hesed,* and everywhere she goes *hesed* is set in motion. In *Ruth* God takes the commonplace and makes it uncommon. Where is God's presence located? It is enmeshed in ordinariness.

God's grace always comes from unexpected places. When we look for it to the right, it comes from the left. When we search to the left, it arrives from the right. In the Book of Ruth, grace comes from a young woman, an astonishing enough fact for that patriarchal culture; and to make it even more astonishing, it comes from a *foreign* woman. Here a Moabite girl teaches the Jews what their God is like. Grace comes not as we expect or as we deserve, but into our need, for that is where God's presence finds a place.

Act 1: Tragedy

Act 1 begins with a series of tragedies. Because of famine in Bethlehem, Elimelech traveled to Moab with his wife Naomi and their two sons. Fleeing death, however, they ran into death. First Elimelech died, leaving Naomi with her two sons. The sons took Moabite wives, Orpah and Ruth, but ten years later both sons died. Now the widow Naomi was left with two grieving daughters-in-law. Much like the story of Job, the story of Ruth begins in unrelenting tragedy.

Act 2: Homecoming

As Act 2 begins, Naomi has decided to leave Moab and return to Bethlehem. The famine is over now, and she is heading home with her two daughters-in-law, Orpah and Ruth. Along the way she stops and tries to persuade them to return to Moab. Her first speech introduces the key theme—God's *hesed* is experienced through human *hesed,* God's kindness comes in human kindness.

She said to them: "Go, return each to her mother's house./May Yahweh do with you the same kindness (hesed)/Which you have done for the dead and for me" (1:8).[2]

She kissed them good-bye, but they refused to leave. Then she said, No, turn back, I am too old to have more sons; and even if by some fluke I could have more sons, by the time they would be old enough to marry you, you'd be old enough for Medicare. No, turn back. I am bad luck. Things are bitter for me. "Indeed, the hand of Yahweh has come out against me" (1:13).

With that speech, Orpah returned home. But Ruth decided to go on with Naomi and spoke those famous words: "Do not press me to abandon you,/To turn back from following you./For wherever you go, I will go;/Where you lodge, I will lodge./Your people become my people;/Your God is now my God" (1:16).

That is *hesed*.

The courage of that decision to forsake home and go with Naomi is virtually unmatched in Scriptures. Phyllis Tribble says: "Not even Abraham's leap of faith surpasses this decision of Ruth's."³ Abraham had the prerogatives of being a male, having family and possessions, and having received a direct word from God. Ruth went on without security, family, and possessions and did so with no vision, no word from God, and no promise of blessing. An astounding leap of faith.

The last scene of this act is the homecoming at Bethlehem. It should have been happiness and joy, but Naomi is mired in grief. Her grief casts a shadow of gloom over the scene.

As Naomi and Ruth hit town, the women ran excitedly to welcome Naomi home. "Naomi," they squealed, "is it really you, Naomi?"

But Naomi answered them: "Do not call me Naomi—that means Sweet One. Call me Mara, the Bitter One. For Shadday-God has made me bitter indeed. I was full when I went away, but God has brought me back *empty*. My husband and sons are dead. So don't call me Sweet One, call me Bitter. God the Judge has testified against me. Shadday-God has sentenced me to misery." (See 1:20-21.)

Her grief is lodged in bitterness and anger, which is where grief often lodges. And haven't we felt like her when tragedy strikes? Suddenly a wave sweeps over us, and inexplicably we feel guilty and accused and cry out, "What have I done?" We wonder if God is punishing us. We know better in our heads, but our insides tighten and we cry out, "What have I done?" I don't know whether to call what sweeps over us sick religion or childish religion or primitive religion (psychiatrists call it the childhood myth of omnipotence[4]), but whatever it is or whatever we name it, sweep over us it does. God is seen as Judge.

Interestingly, Naomi calls God "Shadday" here—an ancient primitive name for God still used in Canaan long after Yahweh had given his name to Moses. Had she dredged this old name for God up from childhood religion and the childhood fears of an angry God? Who knows? It is clear, however, that for Naomi, God is Judge; and in the face of such a God, what can she do but sink deeper and deeper into depression? Anger turns inward. Grief gets lodged.

The homecoming is spoiled by the bitterness of grief. It is harvesttime, however, and this sets the stage for the next act.

Act 3: Gleaning in the Sheaves

Act 3 begins with the two women. As Naomi slumps in passivity, Ruth takes the initiative; she goes to the fields to glean. There was a law in ancient Israel designed to help the poor. The harvesters were not to clean up all the loose barley and wheat after they had harvested the crop. The gleanings were left for the poor to gather. This was before "supply-side economics," and God made built-in provisions for the poor.

Ruth went to glean some of the loose barley. As luck would have it she arrived at the field owned by Boaz. Or was it luck? God stays in the shadows all through the story, but He is always acting—this time through the "coincidence" of Ruth going to the field owned by Boaz.

Boaz was close kin to Naomi. In addition, he was a wealthy man. The attractive, foreign Ruth caught the eye of Boaz and he asked who she was. The workers told him the story of how she had come to Bethlehem with her mother-in-law, Naomi.

Boaz went over to her, welcomed her to stay in his fields, and proceeded to give her the red carpet treatment. He instructed the workers to drop a little extra grain for her. When Ruth asked why he was treating her, a foreigner, so well, Boaz replied: "[I have heard of all you have done for Naomi. For your kindness may you be rewarded by God] *under whose wings you have come to seek refuge"* (2:12). Remember that line. Boaz will.

The contagion of kindness. The *hesed* of Ruth brings out *hesed* from Boaz. Love begets love.

Then Ruth bowed and said, "May I continue to find favor in your eyes, my lord./Because you have comforted me/And because you have spoken to the heart of your maid-servant" (2:13). The sparks have begun to fly!

That night Ruth returned with a big bag of barley and some extra bread which Boaz had given her. Naomi was amazed: "Where did you get all that?" "I went to the field of Boaz," Ruth replied. Naomi was impressed. She now begins to come to life. Her grief begins to break. Her speech moves from cursing to blessing. God's image changes from Judge to Giver of life, and Naomi moves from passivity to activism.

Naomi said of Boaz' kindness: "Blessed be he by Yahweh/Who has not forsaken his *hesed*/With the living and the dead" (2:20 *a*). Then she explained to Ruth that Boaz was a close relation to the family: "He is one of our circle of redeemers" (v. 20 *b*).

What did she mean? As one of the extended family Boaz could exercise responsibility for these two widows. That is what *redemption* means in the Old Testament—*to take responsibility for.* It has an earthy, commonsense, everyday meaning. To redeem someone is to take responsibility for him, to take care of him.

The compassion of Boaz begins to bring Naomi out of grief. How remarkably the theme speaks again. Ruth showed *hesed* toward Naomi. Boaz sees this and responds with *hesed* toward Ruth. Now the *hesed* of Boaz brings Naomi out of bitterness, grief, and passivity. As her grief breaks, she moves to blessing, joy, and action. Ruth has begun a contagious chain reaction of kindness.

Act 4: Encounter at the Threshing Floor

This act happens amid darkness and shadows. It begins as Naomi moves into action. Naomi perceived what Boaz and Ruth perhaps refused to admit—that romance was brewing. Why, Boaz was old enough to be Ruth's father! Could it be? Naomi also knew the rules of levirate marriage: if a man died without children, a kinsman could take the widow as his wife and help her bear children. The purpose of it was twofold: to carry on the family name and to provide protection for widows.

So, moving to action, Naomi concocted a plan. It was designed to force the action and to put the wheels of matrimony into motion. She counseled Ruth: "Boaz is at the threshing floor tonight working with the grain. Bathe yourself, anoint yourself, and go there tonight. After he has finished eating and drinking and lies down for the night, go lie down at his feet. He will tell you what to do." (See 3:3-5.)

Obediently, Ruth went. She arrived at the threshing floor. Full of food and drink, Boaz had gone to sleep. Ruth came in, lifted the covers about his feet, and lay down. About midnight Boaz was startled and reached for his covers. Lo and behold, he discovered a woman. "Who are you?" he said, startled in the darkness. "I am Ruth, your maid-servant" (3:9*a*). And then Ruth *proposed to him* —right there on the spot! She said, "Now spread your 'wing' over your maid-servant, for you are a redeemer" (3:9).

She called his hand: "The first day we met you said, 'May God spread His wings over you.' Well, practice what you preach. Spread your wings over me, or to use the vernacular, 'Boaz, marry me.'"

The midnight scene is masterfully crafted. It is full of suggestiveness about what could have happened. But the story makes it clear. Whatever dishonorable there was that could have happened did not happen. This night was to be a night of honor. Living as God's people means a determination that things be done honorably. This whole book is about the righteous and responsible life. The encounter at the threshing floor was no exception. And, honorable man that Boaz was, he did nothing to take advantage of her.

What did Boaz say—interrupted in the middle of the night by a woman saying, "Marry me"? He said, "Blessed may you be by Yahweh, my daughter./You have made your latter hesed/Better than the former" (3:10). He was saying, "The *hesed* you show me is even better than that shown Naomi, for you have preferred this old man over all the younger men around here. So do not fear, my daughter; I will take care of you, for you are a worthy woman."

Then Boaz introduced a bit of suspense in the story, saying: "Now it is certainly true that I am a redeemer [meaning a kinsman who could take responsibility for her]. But there is another kinsman closer in line, who by law must first decide whether to marry you. So, lodge here for the night and tomorrow I will see that you are taken care of. If he will not redeem you, I shall" (see vv. 12-13).

So she stayed till just before daybreak. Boaz then sent her to Naomi under the cover of darkness with a shawl full of grain.

When Ruth got home she told Naomi what had happened, then gave her some grain and said, "[Boaz gave me this for you. For he told me], "You shall not go empty to your mother-in-law" (3:17).

Now Naomi's grief was healed. She demonstrated a new confidence in God who is no longer Judge, but is now Giver of Life. She said to Ruth, "Just sit tight, my daughter, don't fret. Things will work out, for Boaz will not rest until he has accomplished what he set out to do." (See 3:18.)

Act 5: Resolution at the City Gate

Boaz was true to his word. He went up to the city gate where business was always transacted. Just then the kinsman closer in line came by. He gave the man the opportunity to redeem Elimelek's land and to marry Ruth. Boaz said, "Tell me if you will be the redeemer. If you won't, I shall" (see 4:4).

The man wanted the land but not the responsibility for Ruth, so he declined. Therefore, before ten witnesses, Boaz executed the legal covenant to buy the land and marry Ruth.

All who went around the gate joined in a blessing: "May Yahweh make Ruth like Leah and Rachel and give to Boaz the power to father children" (see 4:12). Because Ruth had been barren the ten years of her first marriage and because Boaz was just a few years short of Social Security, it was no idle prayer.

Act 6: A Baby Boy!

The last act is all joy and excitement. Boaz and Ruth are blessed with a son.

The spotlight, however, turns from the happy couple to an even happier Naomi. The story which began in tragedy for Naomi now ends in joy. It began in death and ends in new life. The empty, bitter Mara is now full and happy Naomi again.

Ruth gave her son to Naomi so Naomi could be his nurse. The

women of Bethlehem gathered around Naomi and said: "[Blessed be Yahweh who has provided a redeemer for you. This child will be a life-restorer, one who will sustain you in your old age. And as for Ruth, your daughter-in-law, who loves you and has borne the son], *she means more to you than seven sons!*" (4:14-15). What an extraordinary comment for that patriarchal world where sons were always more highly valued than daughters! The women's cries close the book: "A son is born to Naomi" (v. 17).

Conclusion

Those are the last words spoken in this story, but God's story goes on and on. At the end of the Book of Ruth, there is a genealogy—a family tree.

Obed, the son born to Ruth and Boaz, had a son named Jesse who had a son named David. King David. Imagine that! King David had foreign blood in his veins, the blood of a Moabite woman named Ruth who taught the Jews what their God was like, a woman who gave us a picture of the *hesed* of God, that nurturing love of God perhaps best embodied in the feminine. There are some dimensions of God that a woman best represents.

Of course, even that's not all of the story. Matthew gives us the genealogy of Jesus, and we discover that Ruth was not only in David's family tree but in Jesus' family tree as well.

If you look at Jesus' family tree you will see heroic figures like Abraham and David, shady, weak figures like Jacob, a prostitute named Rahab, an adulteress named Bathsheba, and a Moabite girl named Ruth.

O the mystery of God's grace. How He works through the good and bad within each of us. How He works with the proud and mighty, the lowly and humble. How He takes the commonplace and makes it uncommon. How He took a bereft widow named Ruth and made her the foremother of Christ. How He took a hole-in-the-wall village named Bethlehem and made it a place of *hesed*. How He took that same village one thousand years later and made it the center of the universe as a star stood in homage to a child nestled there in the straw, a child who would become the Redeemer and one day, for all time, take responsibility for us all.

Notes

1. *The Worship Book* (The Westminster Press, Philadelphia, 1970), pp. 167-75. In a new updating of the lectionary, Ruth has been included.
2. All translations as cited come from Edward F. Campbell, Jr., in his extraordinary commentary—*Ruth,* The Anchor Bible, Vol. 7 (New York: Doubleday & Co., 1975).
3. Phyllis Tribble, *God and the Rhetoric of Sexuality* (Philadelphia: Fortress Press, 1978), p. 173.
4. Psychiatrists call such a reaction the vestiges of the childhood myth of omnipotence. Early on we believe that everything and everyone in life revolves around our wishes. Everything that happens is the result, we think, of the strings we pull. Only the brute facts of reality teach us different, but the myth within persists. When tragedy strikes it speaks its lines in us.

14
The Rich Man and Lazarus

Some parables Jesus told with a glow of God's love in His face. Others He told with tear-brimmed eyes. The story of the rich man and Lazarus is one of the latter. It was told first to the Pharisees. "Lovers of money," Jesus called them. The Pharisees believed that one's riches were a sign of one's own righteousness and of God's blessing, a flawed theology which Calvinism would reincarnate much later in America.

The parable is a drama of the kingdom of God reversing things on earth. Mary sang of it in the Magnificat: "He has put down the mighty from their thrones/and exalted those of low degree;/he has filled the hungry with good things,/and the rich he has sent empty away" (Luke 1:52-53). Jesus spoke of it in the Lukan Beatitudes: "Blessed are you poor, for yours is the kingdom of heaven. . . . But woe to you that are rich, for you have received your consolation. . . . Blessed are you that hunger now, for you shall be satisfied. . . . Woe to you that are full now, for you shall hunger (Luke 6:20-21,24-25).

This parable couldn't be more pertinent today. The dominant secular religions of our day have to do with economics—with why the rich are rich and the Lazaruses are poor. The religions of Karl Marx and Adam Smith are locked in mortal combat and the poor of the world are losers in both. We're witnessing a collision course set between the rich and the poor. The clash could be fatal. The answer isn't in the ideologies of Marx or Smith. The answer is the kingdom of God. So perhaps it's time to listen to this parable again.

The story's opening scene is a vivid picture. The rich man is called Dives in Christian tradition. It's the stock name for a rich man. Rockefeller has the same ring today. Dives was dressed in a custom-tailored suit. Evening meals were a formal affair with white tie and tux, silver, candles, crystal, and china. A before-dinner drink was followed by a cocktail, followed by onion soup. Next came the salad with rich blue cheese dressing. Beef Wellington was the entree, served, of course, with a vintage wine and accompanied by a baked potato and fresh asparagus. Dessert was sumptuous: cherries jubilee and a hot cup of coffee.

But his lavish spread is marred by something—an unsightly man lying at his gate—a poor man, a beggar named Lazarus. The name ironically meant "God helps." In the eyes of many people, this name was a joke. Here, the poor, ugly, and diseased man is named "God helps!" "You've got to be kidding!" "If God helps *him*, who wants God? I can do without that kind of help, thank you!" But to Jesus and to Luke and to those who understood the gospel, the name was, oh, so right. Right, because there's a special place in God's heart for the poor, the slaves, the hurting, the forgotten, and the downtrodden. Always has been. Much earlier God had shown His hand and His heart by siding with a small group of slaves in Egypt. He hadn't changed sides. His special people still were made up with the likes of Lazarus. That's the biblical bias—God is on the side of the poor.

Lazarus mars the picture. He sits at the rich man's gate hoping just for a few scraps from the table to fall his way: perhaps those scraps the rich man dropped accidentally; perhaps the pieces of bread the rich would use to wipe their hands on at the table and then throw away. (Supply-side economics isn't new! The "trickle down" theory has been around for ages!)

Not only is Lazarus hungry, he's also sick, covered with sores: and to add insult to injury, dogs come up and lick his sores. To the pain of sickness is added its humiliation. What's worse than to have to suffer your sickness in public?

Dives is probably not a bad man; he's a religious person. But he doesn't even see Lazarus. Luke is not surprised—neither is Jesus. His stories make the point over and over again. Riches don't damn a person—but they do make salvation more difficult. Affluence offers spiritual dangers. Our hearts sometimes grow cold and hard when our pocketbooks grow fat and heavy. The rich person doesn't always see the poor person. There's a commuter train from rich Westchester County to the business section of New York City. It is interesting to see what happens as it passes through Harlem. Up go the *Wall Street Journals* and *New York Times.* No one sees Harlem, only yesterday's closing prices and today's hot tips. No one looks at Lazarus. He's not easy to look at. He reminds us of what we once were, or what we might have been, or what could happen, God help us. Lazarus. "Out of sight, out of mind," the saying goes. No one looks at Harlem; our heads turn from Lazarus.

We hear Jesus' story differently than many of Jesus' followers did when He first told it. Many of them were pretty poor themselves. They rooted for Lazarus and booed the rich man.

Lazarus was them. The roles have changed today. Helmut Gollwitzer, a German theologian, gave a recent book a title that tells the whole story—*Rich Christian and Poor Lazarus*. Makes us wince, doesn't it? We've faced the statistics—America, Christian America is 6 percent of the world's population consuming one-third of the world's goods. In relation to the rest of the world, we, with Europe and Japan, *are* the rich man, and Lazarus is that Third World we'd just as soon not see on the 7 o'clock news. Can we hear the story properly without seeing that Dives is us—rich and religious us?

But we identify with Lazarus, too, don't we? It may be the Lazarus we were "back when," in the depression or before we made it. No matter what our income is, there are always the rich above us, ignoring us, angering us with their extravagance. But we dare not psychologize this parable away. Nobody here is so poor that there's not someone lying at our gate hoping for what we throw away. Our inclination is to identify with Lazarus. But Jesus looks at the Pharisees and us and says: Lazarus is not you. He's the one lying at our gate.

The story moves on; they both die. But Lazarus is carried by the angels to rock his soul in the bosom of Abraham, while the rich man goes to meet his judgment in that less desirable place.

The rich man's torment consisted in *where he was* and *what he*

The Rich Man and Lazarus

saw. Where he was was in a great deal of discomfort, and what he saw was the pain of separation—there at a distance with a great gulf in between was his spiritual father Abraham with his arms around *Lazarus.* Now he saw Lazarus!

I don't know what hurt the rich man more: the room temperature or the sight of Lazarus whooping it up with Abraham. (There was Lazarus filling up with T-bone steaks and eating mountains of ice cream.) The rich man calls out, "*Father* Abraham"—remember, he was a good Jew who thought himself to be a child of Abraham, an heir of Abraham's promise.

"Please have mercy. Send Lazarus to dip the end of his finger in water and cool my tongue. I'm in torment."

Abraham replies, "My child, remember that while you were alive, you had the good things—the good jobs, the good schools, good streets, good houses, good food—while Lazarus only got leftovers, if he was lucky. But now the tables are turned. He's got it made and you're the one gone begging" (see Luke 16:24-25).

James Sanders once translated Abraham's response for a congregation in Harlem this way: "Listen son, Lazarus ain't running no more errands for you." Incredible, isn't it? Even in torment the rich man still considered Lazarus his errand boy. There's a name for that: "invincible ignorance."

But Abraham was not through. "On top of this," he said, "someone has dug a great gulf between us so that no one can get from your side to mine or my side to yours" (see v. 26). Jesus wasn't interested in telling us who dug the ditch. But it couldn't be God. He sent His Son to try to bridge that gulf. While those whom Jesus called "lovers of money" were plotting to kill Him, He was preparing to die for them. That ditch was dug long before the rich man died. It reached from the rich man's house to eternal dwelling places. Dives dug it with his turned head and tight fist, with his jokes and votes.

The story doesn't stop here, however. The rich man is persistent —he didn't get rich by being a quitter. He makes another proposal —this one less selfish.

"Well then, Father Abraham, will you please send him to my father's house where my five brothers live? Let Lazarus warn them so they won't end up here with me."

It was a reasonable request, even an honorable one. Jesus' hearers would have expected Abraham to grant it. Similar stories of that time had the happy endings. God would surely grant that! He *is* in the saving business, after all.

We're shocked to hear Abraham's response: "No, no deal. Your brothers have Moses and the prophets, let them hear *them.*"

Dives keeps trying: "No, Father, they won't listen to them. But if someone goes to them from the dead, they will repent."

Abraham replies for the last time. "If they don't hear Moses and the prophets, neither will they be convinced if someone should rise from the dead" (see vv. 28-31).

That's the end. The focus has changed, startlingly, from Dives and Lazarus *to the five brothers,* and to us—we who are still living, who watch the rich people and the Lazaruses, who sit in church and hear sermons on this parable. It's to us, the living, that Jesus now turns. What will we do about the way we live and how we treat our neighbor? Center stage, now, for the five brothers.

Abraham addresses *us:* "You have the Bible and the preachers; listen to *them.*" He catches us in a subtle danger. How evasive and all too easy it is to demand from God a special sign, or special word, or new experience in order for us to respond to Him.

Jesus rebuked those of His day who, like spoiled children or cynical spectators, demanded signs and miracles from God. "You won't get a sign," Jesus warned them, "except the sign of Jonah" —the word of the prophet (see Matt. 12:39).

It's an old and familiar game we play with God. We demand a new word from the Lord, while ignoring the Word he's already given. We preoccupy ourselves with strange and mysterious texts while ignoring the plain and simple ones. I like Mark Twain's honesty: "It's not the parts of the Bible I do *not* understand that give me trouble; it's the parts of the Bible I *do* understand."

God hasn't withheld His word about how we're to live. The Ten Commandments teach the love of God and neighbor just as Jesus did. The Psalms teach rulers to take care of the poor and helpless. The prophets relay God's rebuke to the rich who exploit the poor. Jesus told us salvation has to do with a cup of water and a gift of food.

We are the five brothers who have Moses and the prophets and the gospel. We've heard the preachers and the teachers. We've been given "a lamp unto [our] feet, a light unto [our] path" (Ps. 119-105). What will we do with it?

We may respond to God's word. If so, it will open our eyes, soften our hearts, and extend our hands to our neighbor. The kingdom will then be in our midst in new and wonderful ways.

But we may sit like a spoiled child and petulantly demand more—seek signs, a miracle, a proof. If we are in the latter group, the story draws the curtain down in judgment.

Albert Schweitzer was changed by the reading of this parable. He saw that Africa was poor Lazarus sitting at Europe's doorstep. He left his sumptuous table in Europe and founded his hospital in Lambarene. In his most famous book, he concluded that there is one way to know Jesus—and that way is to hear His command "Follow me" and to follow Him in obedience.

We may demand more—a new vision of Jesus, another resurrection, a tender, warm experience. But Jesus and Luke and Abraham and Schweitzer know better. We are not transformed by seeing a miracle. That's *cheap faith*. We are transformed as we hear God's Word and respond in trust and obedience.

It's ironic that the Jesus who spoke this parable was Himself raised from the dead by God. Was Luke trying to tell us something by including this passage? Was He saying that if we are not transformed by Jesus' life and death, we won't be transformed by His resurrection?

When Jesus was raised that Easter morning, He appeared not to his enemies as if to spite them, not to those demanding a sign so to convince them; rather, He appeared to those who loved Him, who had pledged to follow Him, so to confirm them and strengthen them. That's our promise as we join those who hear and say yes to God's word: Christ comes to us in our obedience.

One of my friends was working his way through seminary as a part-time carpenter. One day before the 1976 presidential election, Stan was working across town with a poor laborer. As could have been expected, politics came up. Stan asked, "Who you gonna vote for?" "Not Jimmy Carter," the man replied. "Why not?" "Because he's a Southern Baptist," the man answered. "What's wrong with voting for a Southern Baptist?" Stan then asked. The man spat back: "Because Southern Baptists don't give a darn for poor people!"

What knocks the breath out of me when I hear that is not just the language, or the anger and hurt there. But it's the thought: just how recently in our own past we were that man—we were Lazarus—and now we're the five brothers of Dives. We have moved, in one or two generations, from poor white folk to the comfortable establishment in the South. This offers for us a new spiritual test. We, like Jesus, are in a wilderness trying to decide who we are and *whose* we are.

The parable calls us to repentance and obedience. What that repentance and obedience looks like may not be clear now. But the call to befriend the poor is unmistakably clear.

As we open ourselves to God's Spirit, we'll find what to do. It may be responding more fully to world hunger relief offerings. It may be working for political solutions to the hunger problem. It may mean lowering our standard of living so that we can minister more fully to those around us. Some have chosen professions that help the poor. Some have made adjustments so their professions can serve the poor and not just the "well heeled."

If our mission thrust is to be bold and not just *brash*, then we need to reach not for other church's members, but to the poor of the earth; we need to care for those who may never join our rolls or give us something in return. In short, we need to care about Lazarus.

It catches us up short, doesn't it—we brothers and sisters of Dives? Don't expect any more word from God than this. Don't expect any signs or miracles.

For if we won't listen to Moses and the prophets, we won't believe one who has risen from the grave—we won't even believe the One who *did* rise from the grave.

15
Zacchaeus and Jesus:
The Day the Camel Passed Through the Needle's Eye

The day began as any other day. Zacchaeus rolled out of his satin sheets, slipped his robe over his silk pajamas, and weaved his way across the marble floor to the bathroom. Mounting the step stool, he climbed two steps to where he could see himself in the mirror. "Cursed house," he muttered, "built by giants." Then he looked at his tired old face and rubbed his bloodshot eyes. Another long, lonely night of drinking. *I've got to stop that,* he said to himself for the hundredth time. Then he gulped down a couple of aspirin, swallowing the water as quietly as he could.

Zacchaeus was his name—a noble, thoroughly Jewish name meaning "Righteous One." A tax-collector named "Righteous." Better the town prostitute be named "Chastity." For a Jew to be a tax-collector made him both thief and traitor. He was a thief because he had the unregulated power to gouge his people for as high a tax as he wanted and then could pocket the profit. He was a traitor because here was a son of Abraham working as a lackey for Rome.

Imagine living in the Soviet Union today where Jews are persecuted and oppressed. Then imagine a Jew who decided to become an officer in the Communist government's secret police. That is how his fellow Jews looked upon Zacchaeus. That is why, for all his obvious wealth, he drank alone. Luke reported that he was not only a tax-collector but *chief* tax-collector, and not only

133

chief tax-collector but also *rich*. That word was not incidental to Luke. Just the chapter before, the rich young ruler had gone sorrowfully away when Jesus asked him to sell all he had and give it to the poor. Just the chapter before Jesus had concluded how hard it is for a rich man to enter the kingdom of God—it is easier for a camel to pass through the eye of the needle.

Two strikes against Zacchaeus: he is a tax-collector and rich.

But this day in the life of Zacchaeus was not to be like any other day. Zacchaeus heard that Jesus was coming to Jericho. What happened next unfolds before us the surprise of mercy: *Zacchaeus went to find Jesus and discovered that Jesus was already in search of him.* That is the surprise of mercy, the miracle of grace: before we search for God, God is already in search of us.

Zacchaeus went to see this Jesus. The crowd was already blocking his view of the street—no new problem. What would Zacchaeus do? Fighting back his inclination to retreat, to curse his height or the crowd, Zacchaeus became as a child, scampered up a sycamore tree, and, unwittingly, readied himself to greet the kingdom of God.

The kingdom came in Jesus, who saw Zacchaeus in the tree, walked over to him, called him by name, and said, "Zacchaeus, hurry down that tree, I must go to your house today!" (see v. 5).

The *divine initiative!* Zacchaeus went to see Jesus and Jesus was already in search of him.

Isn't that the way God is? Haven't you been in Zacchaeus's shoes? You finally decided to do something about your life, to change a few things, and you discover that God has already been at work in you. You may have given up on God, but He has not given up on you. God has been around all the while searching, prompting, waiting.

One great hymn speaks to the mystery of the divine initiative that we perceive only perhaps after we have come to him: "I sought the Lord, and afterward I knew/He moved my soul to seek Him, seeking me;/It was not I that found, O Saviour true;/No, I was found of Thee."

That was when salvation dawned for Zacchaeus: when Jesus called him by name, stuck up His hand, and invited Himself for dinner. That is how the salvation of God in Christ begins—in the glad welcome of God.

I would like to have seen the expression on Zacchaeus's face when Jesus walked up and invited Himself to dinner. Frederick Buechner says: "It is not reported how Zacchaeus got out of the sycamore, but the chances are good that he fell out in pure astonishment."[1]

In those days to go to someone's house and share a meal was reserved for the best of friends. Jesus was not saying, "Sinner, I want an appointment with you, now!" It was more like, "Friend, let's go have lunch."

That is how salvation dawns for us too. God moves near in Jesus and extends His welcoming arms. No matter who you are or what you have done, God welcomes you into His kingdom. And He keeps coming, He keeps extending those arms, until we decide that it is *God's* salvation that we want, that it is *God's* salvation which is the only one that really counts.

Enter the grumblers. Here is the dark side of the story: While one person is being saved, others grow angry and begin their plots to kill Jesus. How can this Jesus be so free with God's love?

When Jesus walked up to Zacchaeus the crowd leaned forward, licking their lips in anticipation, waiting for Jesus to preach Zacchaeus hellfire and damnation. Woe unto you; repent. Shape up or else. Give it to him, Jesus!

But what they heard was Jesus saying, "Hey, Zacchaeus, hurry down that tree; I'm staying with you today." You could have heard a pin drop. Then the murmuring and grumbling began: "He has gone in to be the guest of a man who is a sinner" (v. 7).

Like Jonah seeing Nineveh spared, like the elder brother watching his no-account brother's homecoming feast, like the Pharisees of all ages who claim God's love for themselves and limit it for certain others, the fine citizens of Jericho were not one bit happy with Jesus. The thought of it: Jesus inviting Himself as a guest of Zacchaeus, that traitor, that thief, that chief of sinners, that foreshortened excuse for a human being!

So off the crowd goes grumbling and plotting, and off go Zacchaeus and Jesus, one just down from a tree, the other about to be nailed to a tree, to Zacchaeus's home for dinner.

And there at Zacchaeus's house salvation was completed. If it always begins with God's first move, it necessarily ends in human response. And the response has concrete, life-altering consequences. Salvation begins in the eternity of heaven, but it is completed in the everydayness of earth.

For Zacchaeus it was *conversion* in the strictest sense of the word—an about-face. It was *repentance* in the strictest sense of the word—a change of mind and heart. Zacchaeus said: "Look, *Lord* [note Jesus had become *Lord*], half of all I have I will give to the poor; for everybody I have cheated I will repay 400 percent" (see v. 8).

Salvation moves us from the arithmetic of the law to the extravagance of grace. The law said the most you need give to the poor was 20 percent—Zacchaeus gave 50 percent. And the law said all you need pay back someone you cheated was the principal plus 20 percent—Zacchaeus gave back 400 percent.

The servants overhearing Zacchaeus probably fainted. Here was a *new creation!* Walter Rauschenbusch commented: "Here a camel passed through the needle's eye and Jesus stood and cheered."[2]

"Today," Jesus said, "salvation has come to this house" (v. 9). The salvation that began in heaven was completed on earth; what began in the heart of God reached into the bank account of Zacchaeus. What began as the initiative of grace ended in the repentance of Zacchaeus.

Isn't that how God's salvation in Christ operates? It does not require prior repentance, else it would not be grace. It comes bringing repentance in its wings. In God's gospel welcome precedes worthiness, acceptance comes before change. As John Claypool put it in a sermon on Zacchaeus: "Acceptance is the condition of change; change is not the condition of acceptance."

Zacchaeus received the salvation of God—the only free thing he had ever received—and this salvation worked repentance in him. Three cheers for Zacchaeus.

"*Today*," Jesus said, "I must go to your house." "*Today*," he said, "salvation has come to this house."

Today is the tense of salvation. It is also its urgency. "Today I *must* go to your house." If salvation is available *now,* what could be more important?

Salvation comes to you in the "Eternal now" of God. The gospel of Christ celebrates the present tense of salvation. *Now* is the acceptable time of the Lord. *Today* Scripture is fulfilled in your hearing. "Behold, *now* is the acceptable time; behold, *now* is the day of salvation" (2 Cor. 6:2, KJV).

Today, now, this moment, in the preaching of this Word, the kingdom draws near. God's saving power is available to you now—in whatever ways you most need it: the power to forgive, the power to be sustained, the power to let go of that which enslaves you, the power to ward off temptation, the power to believe. God's salvation even now draws near.

Saint Augustine prayed as a young man, "Lord, make me good, but *not yet.*" Those words, *not yet,* defy the todayness of God's salvation.

How is God wishing to change you this day? Do not let the particulars of Zacchaeus's conversion put you off. Salvation is not a legalism; it is life in the Spirit of God. It is not a matter of what you *have* to do. It is a matter of what you offer to God in response to His love.

Just take, for example, the contrast between Zacchaeus and the rich young ruler. Jesus demanded that the rich young ruler sell *all* that he had and give it to the poor. Zacchaeus got off with giving away only *half.* Did the rich young ruler get a bad deal?

How come the inconsistency? That inconsistency marks the difference between life under the law and life under grace.

The rich young ruler said, "What do I *have* to give up to be saved?" (see 18:18). That is the voice of the law. And Jesus said to him, "You have to give it all." Zacchaeus said, "Lord, here is half of all I have; I offer it to you and the kingdom." That is the voice touched by grace. And Jesus stood and cheered. "Zacchaeus, salvation has come to your house *today*."

Almighty and gracious God, Whose Son came to seek and save the lost, come now to us in our lostness, our loneliness, our sin, and our sickness that we may be found of Thee. Then we will turn to Thee and to our neighbor with love, then we will hear salvation's bell ring out, today, today, today, grace has come. To the praise of Thy glory. Through Jesus Christ our Lord, Amen.

Notes

1. Frederick Buechner, *Wishful Thinking* (New York: Harper & Row, 1973), p. 100.
2. Walter Rauschenbusch, *The Social Principles of Jesus* (New York: Association Press, 1921), p. 68.

16
Revelation:
The End of the Story

It is important to know how God's Story begins: with a Creator God who scooped us out of the clay, blew into us His own breath, and called us good.

It is important to know the crux of the Story, the climax: when God became a man named Jesus who died on a Roman cross to show us a love so high and so broad and so deep that not even this death could stop God from loving us.

But it is also important to know how the Story ends.

David Buttrick tells the story of a family whose guest room was always filled with guests. One day the children in the family played a practical joke. They sneaked into the guest room, took the mystery novel off the bedside table, tore out the last chapter, and returned the book to its place.

The next morning the guest came to the breakfast table bleary-eyed and curious. What happened to the last chapter? How did it turn out? "Who-dun-it?" He went home, found the mystery in a second-hand book store, and finished it. To his great surprise, some things he thought were important turned out to be irrelevant and some things he had ignored became most important in the end.

In the same way, we need to read the last chapter of God's story. "For," as David Buttrick says,

> If God's story will end in a world reconciled, with New Humanity engaged in grave, glad courtesies of love, with "the sound of them that triumph and the shout of them that feast," with the

City and the Lamb and wiped away tears, then all our stories must be revised.[1]

The story comes from the very mind and heart of God to a man named John. He is a prophet and a prisoner. (Many times the two go together.) Because he has refused to bow down and worship Rome and call Caesar Domitian "Lord," John is banished from Ephesus and imprisoned on an island named Patmos. And his brothers and sisters in Christ, whom he had to leave in Asia Minor, are in great danger. If they refuse to bow down they too risk persecution, imprisonment, and even death.

John is consumed with terrifying questions. Why is Domitian so powerful? Why does God allow the forces of evil to be so strong? Why does He let evil persons prosper and good people be persecuted? Who is in control after all? Who will win out? What is to happen to the churches?

And God gave John a story. It came from visions brought by an angel. It is a wild, fantastic story filled with terrifying animals and mysterious persons, glimpses of heaven and hell, and darkness and light.

The story occurs on two levels. On the first level it is a survival document for a persecuted church. It is God's message to the downtrodden. It is a secret document written in codes—an animal code, a number code, and a color code; it is an underground document written to reveal the meaning of history to the persecuted people of faith and to hide it from the persecutors. At this level it has been an important word from God to the persecuted church throughout the centuries.

But, on a deeper level, it taps a region deeper than the mind, a land of archetypes and symbols where God still walks with us in the cool of the day.

At its most profound level this is a child's story, a story intended for the child in each of us. Lest this diminish its importance, remember, Jesus said, "Unless you . . . become like children you shall not enter the kingdom of heaven" (Matt. 18:3, NASB).

In some ways it resembles those children's stories called fairy tales—like *Alice in Wonderland,* Tolkien's *Lord of the Rings,* or even *Star Wars.*

With one big difference! These others came from the imagination of men; this one came from the very mind of God. This story is true, the truest story in the world. It tells a truth too good not to be true, because it comes from a God whose goodness is beyond our imaginings.

We call the story *Revelation.* In it terrible things happen and wonderful things happen. It tells of a world where the forces of light wage mortal combat against the forces of darkness, yet where the darkness does not overcome the light. The victory finally belongs to God, regardless of how dark it looks at times.

It is a struggle in which, despite all our costumes and masquerades, the true identities of the heroes and villains are revealed. In the end the battle goes to the good and, to quote Buechner, "everybody, good and evil alike, becomes known by his true name."[2] It affirms God's final victory and gives us a "fleeting glimpse of Joy, Joy beyond the walls of the world."[3]

But enough *about* the story. Hear now the story.

It begins in heaven—at God's throne. That's where everything always begins. That is where the universe began and stars were flung into space. That is where history begins—and ends. As one great historian, Herbert Butterfield, put it: "If God stopped breathing we would all vanish."

It all begins at God's throne, and that's where the story begins. John sees the throne and the face of God gleams like all the jewels in the world shining together. Around the throne are twenty-four elders singing songs of praise. And four strange flying creatures—one like a lion, one like a bull, and one with a man's face, and one like an eagle—all four are flying around the throne beating their wings and singing, "Holy, Holy, Holy."

Then there appears a Lamb. He has been killed but is yet alive. We know His secret name—it is Jesus Christ. Thousands, no, millions break forth in joyous song: "Worthy is the Lamb that was slain to receive power and riches, and wisdom, and strength, and honour and glory, and blessing" (5:12, KJV). The Lamb goes to the throne and takes a scroll on which is written all of history. The scroll is bound together by seven seals, and now the Lamb begins to break open the seals.

As the scroll opens you see history happening before your eyes, history you know like the back of your hand.

First we see the white horse of conquering and on that horse we see a parade of conquerors: Alexander the Great, Julius Caesar, Napoleon, Hitler, and on and on.

Then we see a red horse of war. Its rider has a sword and on the sword is the blood of a thousand wars: the Trojan Wars, Gallic Wars, civil wars, World Wars, Vietnam, Afghanistan, El Salvador.

Then comes the black horse of famine, and we see the long, cruel line of parched lips and bloated stomachs from Egypt to Africa to Ireland, to Bangladesh, to Appalachia.

Finally, the fourth horse comes and its color is pale green. It is the horse of death, and on that pale green horse ride plagues and diseases, malaria, smallpox, and cancer.

We know that to be history. Then as all of the seven seals are broken and the scroll is opened up, all of history is unveiled, and we see that it is beset by even more calamity—persecution of Christians, earthquakes, Mount Saint Helen's eruptions, hurricanes washing and wasting, invasions of insects, and on and on. And we are terrified to look and wonder why it is all happening.

Then the story gives us the answer. There has been a revolt against God, and it began in the very throne room of heaven—war in heaven between God's forces and the forces of evil led by a Dragon. Unable to defeat God in heaven the Dragon flees to earth and carries on his war there—against God's people on earth.

You know the secret name of the Dragon: Satan. He is the reason for the revolt and for the chaos and calamity through the course of history.

History is the story of a fight to the finish between the forces of good, led by God, and the forces of evil, led by the Dragon. The forces of heaven are led by a Holy Trinity: God, His Son Jesus Christ, and the Holy Spirit. The forces of darkness are led by three great enemies. The first and foremost has already been introduced: the Dragon. John described him this way: he is a huge, red dragon with a long tail; he has seven heads and on each of the heads are ten horns and a crown.

But the Dragon is not alone. He has two partners in darkness. Just as there is the Holy Trinity there is also an unholy trinity made up of the Dragon, the Beast, and the False Prophet.

The Beast comes from the sea. He also has seven heads and ten horns on each head, and on each horn there is a crown, and on each head there is a name insulting to God. The Dragon gives to the Beast of his own authority and power and throne, and the Beast accepts it. When the Beast from the sea accepts the power and authority from the Dragon, all the world bows down and worships the Beast, saying, "Who is like the Beast?" In the Old Testament that is what the psalmist says about God: "Who is like Jehovah? Who can compare with the Lord?" (see 89:6). You see, the Beast has become like a god! And his number is 666!

Who is the Beast? Anybody or anything that accepts power and authority offered by Satan. Jesus was offered it in the wilderness. But He said no! Each generation has those who say yes.

The Dragon has his partner the Beast, and the Beast changes faces in every generation.

But that is only two. Who is the third member of the unholy trinity? He is the False Prophet—the beast from the land. The False Prophet goes all over the world persuading people to bow down and worship the Beast. He will perform miracles and give gifts; he will use any device available to persuade us to fall down and worship the Beast.

The False Prophet is pictured with two horns like a lamb. He speaks like a dragon and will give you the mark of the Beast if you will fall down and worship him. With that mark you are promised special powers and privileges.

There it is—the story, history—your story and mine. A battle between the Holy Trinity—God, Jesus Christ, and the Holy Spirit—and the unholy trinity—the Dragon, the Beast, and the False Prophet. And the battle is carried on among human beings, those who follow God and those who follow the Dragon. John calls the followers of God "heaven-dwellers," and he calls the followers of the Dragon "earth-dwellers."[4]

The story is true of the *past*. It describes the *present*. But it also unveils the *future*. The title of the Book of Revelation means "unveiling," and that is what God gives us—an unveiling of past and present, and now the *future*.

Who will win? God or the Dragon? Christ or the Beast? The Holy Spirit or the False Prophet? Who is in control? Who will win the final victory?

This is what the story tells: at a time in the future nobody knows—it may be before I finish today, maybe two years, maybe twenty years, maybe even two thousand more years—Christ will return. Only this time He will not come as we first saw Him, the Lamb slain for our sins. This time He will come as a victorious King on a white horse. He will come in power and glory, and on His robe will be written, "King of kings and Lord of lords" (19:16). He will gather all the forces of good and meet all the forces of evil at the final, climactic battle of Armageddon. The battle is fought and Christ wins the battle. Then He throws the Beast and the False Prophet into the lake of fire that burns forever.

The Beast and the False Prophet are taken care of, but there is one member of the unholy trinity left—the Dragon. Now the story is a little like the old Western; it is the final showdown at the OK Corral. While the good guys are taking care of the bad guys, the chief villain escapes and the hero goes after him alone. God Himself, now, goes to take care of the Dragon.

First He sends His angel, and the angel throws the Dragon in a deep pit and chains him there for one thousand years. During that time Christ sets up His kingdom on earth with all God's people. And those all through history who have been killed because they followed Christ, these are brought back to life and rule with Him.

Then the Dragon will make his last-ditch effort to defeat God. God sets him loose, and he goes all over the world and deceives the nations and recruits them to defeat God. The great nations are called Gog and Magog. They gather to defeat God's people, but this time God takes care of them personally. He casts fire from heaven and destroys them, and He throws the Dragon in the lake of fire along with his cohorts in darkness, the Beast and the False Prophet.

Then will come the final judgment when every person shall rise and stand before God. The "earth-dwellers," those who worshiped the Beast and have fought against God, will join the Dragon and the Beast and False Prophet in the lake of fire and suffer what is called "the second death." However, all of those whose names are in the Lamb's Book of Life, each one will be given a smooth, white stone. And on that stone which you will hold in your hand will be written a secret name—perhaps your own secret name, for then you will know yourself completely as only God knows you. Perhaps it is the secret name of Christ, for He will stand by you and for you that day and claim you as His own. God will say, "This stone is your entrance into my Kingdom. Come, enjoy the feast which I have prepared for you since the foundation of the world" (see 2:17).

And then a new heaven and a new earth will appear, replacing the old heaven and earth. The New Jerusalem will come down from heaven, too wonderful to describe in human words. There God will live with us and we with Him. God will wipe away every tear from our eyes and death will be no more. No more tears, no more sickness, no more pain, no more famine, no more war, no more hate, no more sorrow. Every tear will be gone. A river of life will flow through the center of the city. Trees will line both sides of the river which will bear fruit the year around, and we will gather in glad heavenly reunion at God's side around His banquet table and share happily, joyously, hilariously in the feast He has planned for us, His children. Then will be heard "the song of them that triumph and the shout of them that feast."

There the story ends, and John the storyteller turns to you and me and says, in effect: "Do you believe the story? Do you believe it enough to stake your life on it? In the final analysis this is the crucial issue of the book. Not, "Do you understand it all?" or "What is its historical meaning?" or "Who is 666?" or "When is

Christ coming?" or "When is the rapture—before or after?" All these are questions adults argue over because they have lost the child's capacity simply to believe it. John says, "Don't add anything to the story, or leave anything out of it" (see 22:18). He wants us simply to believe it, to hear it, and obey.

When I say, "Do you believe it?" I do not mean, "Do you believe in seven-headed dragons?" I mean: "Do you believe that evil is terrible and real and so is God's judgment on evil?" What I mean is: "Do you really believe that despite appearances sometimes to the contrary, God will conquer all evil and the darkness will not overcome the light?"

The Book of Revelation is, as God's Word often is, a two-edged sword. It cuts two ways. It is warning and it is promise.

The warning is this. You must choose whose side you will join. You must choose today, if you have not already. It makes a difference whose side you are on, a real historical difference and a real eternal difference. So be prepared.

The promise is this: God will win the final victory. Regardless of how it appears, God is in control and His final victory is assured. And you as His children will share the victory. You will be conquerors, too. It may not seem so at times, but God's way will win out. You are on the winning side, not the losing one. Take heart. Hear the promise: God will win the victory.

Have you heard of God's love, that Christ died for you? Have you heard that God's suffering love will finally become a triumphant love? Have you heard and obeyed His invitation to join His side? Have you become a follower of Christ and joined God's people to fight on His side and feed His sheep and love with His love? If so, then you know the Lamb, and the Lamb knows you, your name is in His Book of Life, and this story is a story of great assurance, a glimpse of "Joy—Joy beyond the walls of the world."

"Happy is the one who tells this story, and happy are those who hear the words of the prophecy and obey what is written therein" (see Rev. 1:3).

Notes

1. From a soon to be published manuscript by David Buttrick.
2. Frederick Buechner, *Telling the Truth: The Gospel as Tragedy, Comedy, and Fairy Tale* (New York: Harper & Row, 1977), p. 81.
3. J. R. R. Tolkien, *The Tolkien Reader* (New York: Ballantine, 1966), p. 68.
4. See Paul Minear, *I Saw a New Earth* (Washington: Corpus Books, 1968), p. 261 ff., for his interpretation and translation of "earth-dwellers."

17
The Theology of Narrative Preaching

If you have come to this chapter first you will learn the why and how of narrative preaching and then move to the practical demonstration through sermons. If you have read the sermons first you may have already learned inductively what I say here, and this chapter will help organize what you have observed.

Is there a homiletic, or theology, of narrative preaching? I think so, and it is based upon some primary convictions about preaching.

A Short Homiletic of Narrative Preaching

A preacher must decide what the essence of preaching is.[1] This book is not a comprehensive statement on preaching. It does, however, seek to discern and describe what is the essential core of preaching.

What is preaching? Preaching is the telling of the Biblical Story, the gospel of God's redeeming activity from creation to Christ to consummation. The purpose of preaching is to help the hearer meet the God of the Bible and Jesus Christ, who has shown us God's face, and, having met them, to follow in faith and obedience. The task of preaching is to recreate the biblical world in vividness and truth, the world of history and meaning in which God and His Christ are active, so that the hearer is beckoned to enter it and, as an inhabitant of that world, a child of God, and a disciple of Jesus Christ, to live in God's "righteousing" power and Jesus' power of love.

This opening statement provides the foundation for a homiletic or theology of narrative preaching. Such a homiletic is based upon a view of the nature of God, of humankind, and of the Bible.

God as the God of Creation, History, and Consummation Is a Story-Making God

God's activity in creation, history, and consummation can be described as the Author of the universe writing the story of His life with us. As John Shea puts it: "*We* are the story God tells."[2] Or, as Alfred North Whitehead said, "God is the poet of the world, with tender patience leading it by his vision of truth, beauty and goodness."[3]

Is that not the suggestion of the apostle Paul, who told us: "For we are God's poem (the Greek, *poiema*) created in Christ Jesus for good works which God prepared beforehand, that we should walk in them" (see Eph. 2:10).

God speaks and worlds are made. He tells stories and the drama of life unfolds.

Humankind Is the Creation of God Who Finds Its Meaning in Becoming Part of a Story

We are created to have a story, to discover where we came from, what we are doing—and why—and where we are going.[4] Life has its meaning as it connects with a larger story, and if that story is God's Story, then our lives become part of His salvation story and we ourselves enter the kingdom of God. Abundant life in the kingdom of God is no jangle of meaningless events. Neither is it an endless circle of repeat. Life is going somewhere. It is part of the plot of the providence of God.

Stories tell us who we are. They shape our character and tell us how to behave. Stanley Hauerwas eloquently argues that church is a "story-formed community" whose stories not only give us our identity, but also inform our character.[5] Stories more than rule books shape how we behave.

Having a story, being part of a larger story, also is a crucial resource in dealing with the tragic dimension of life. Oppressed people have used stories and songs to keep hope in bad times.[6] In a recently published essay, hospital chaplain Mark Jensen demonstrates that narrative theology is an important resource in helping cancer patients find their sacred stories and deal constructively with their illness.[7]

The depth psychology of Carl Jung argues that stories offer us passage to the collective unconscious where our deepest self resides and where encounter with God may take place. Stories take us to the place where "deep calls unto deep." There we have the opportunity to be grasped by the Holy God, to wrestle with the angel until the angel blesses us.

Stories help us remember. Samuel Johnson once said that we "more frequently require to be reminded than informed."[8] For the ancient Hebrew (and for us as well) salvation consisted of remembrance, remembrance of God's acts, of who we are and whose we are. Stories are a powerful vehicle of our remembrance. They remind us of what we have forgotten or never personally known or that which, lying deep within, we have never invited up for hearing.

Memory is far more powerful than we moderns normally think. In the ancient concept of memory on which the Passover and the Lord's Supper find their basis, called *anamnesis,* the ancient story is re-presented so that it is brought into the present moment and we take our places among the ancient participants. Such is how Christ can be so real during the Lord's Supper. Such is the power of the biblical stories—the God who acted in the past acts in the present through them.

The Bible Tells the Story of God's Redemptive Work in the World, a Story Which He Compels Us to Enter

The Bible is largely narrative in form. Much of it was told before it was written and heard before it was read. This fact is consistent with the essence of biblical faith—that God is a history-making God and we are His history, that He tells stories, and that we, His people, are His Story. The unique truth of the biblical revelation is its narrative of the ways of God with humankind.[9]

From Genesis to Revelation the Bible tells of our search for God—but more, of God in search of us. In it we see the holiness, righteousness, and love of God at work. In it we see the best and worst of people like you and me.

The Bible is the story of God's purpose, our rebellion against

God's purpose, and God's merciful and self-giving response to our rebellion: the giving up of His son that we and creation might be redeemed. What an astonishment that the God who authored the drama stepped into the drama Himself to act and to be acted upon by the very actors He created, that God would become a suffering God (suffering itself being the act of being acted upon), that His own Son would die at the hands of His own creation in order that redemption could take place.

But, most important of all, it is no mere story of past deeds. It is a living, ongoing drama of redemption. The Holy Spirit works in us to move us to enter the story and become part of it. As we enter it we call God "our Father" and know we can trust Him; we call Jesus Lord and Savior and know He is with us; and we become brothers and sisters to all the people in the Book. As I enter the drama, His Story becomes "my" story and I enter the life-giving stream of God's power and purpose.

So, we join Abraham as he launches out in faith into the unknown country, leaving behind him home, work, and old-time religion. We hear God strike a covenant and say, "Abe, from now on My Story will be your story." We are in the room that day when Abraham and Sarah hear the news. Abraham at 100 and Sarah at 90 are about to be called Daddy and Mommy. Abraham "falls on his face laughing." Sarah overhears while hiding behind a door and doubles over in laughter herself. With one foot in the nursing home and the other in the maternity ward, they shake with faith's laughter and decide to name their son Isaac, which in Hebrew means "laughter."[10] And tears roll down our cheeks at the outrageousness of it all, and our faith is encouraged as we see this faith proved in God, a God who makes good on his promise.

We go to Mount Carmel with the prophet Elijah where God acts in such a visible and dramatic way we feel anyone would be a fool not to believe in God. And we go with the same prophet Elijah, now badly shaken, to Mount Horeb, where God is silent and we wonder whether anyone but a fool could believe in God. We discover with our brother Elijah that our God is a God of words *and* of silence, that He is a God of signs and wonders *and* a God of stillness.

We see our brother David fall into adulterous sins. But he is a man after God's own heart and he loves God as fiercely, joyously, and passionately as any man who ever lived. We see him redeemed and restored and we join him in song: "The Lord is my shepherd, I shall not want" (Ps. 23:1).

We follow young Daniel to a foreign land and watch as he is pressured to disobey the teachings of his faith. This foreign culture, this strange new world is pressuring him to forsake his faith and to make his body impure by eating and drinking from the king's table. We rejoice as he says no to the king's demands, and we gain strength to say no as Daniel becomes our brother.

We see Amos walk into Bethel and hear him thunder a message of judgment: "You disobey God because you ignore the needs of the poor. Your economy exploits the weak; your government protects the rich." And we wince as we hear him speaking to us as well. He not only tells us what is wrong with Bethel—he is telling us what is wrong in Washington and Frankfort and Houston.

We have felt at home in the home of Mary and Martha and watch with bemused recognition as the tension builds between Martha working hard in the kitchen and Mary sitting adoringly at the feet of Jesus. You have felt Peter's tears sting your own cheeks as the cock crows and you realize you have denied Jesus again. You have followed Jesus and disciples at a distance, trying to decide whether to become a disciple. And suddenly Jesus is not asking the disciples, "Who do men say that I am?" He is looking at you and asking, "Who do YOU say that I am?" And you—you have to decide whether or not you will enter the story, join God's people, and be part of God's redemptive work.

We experience the power of God when we enter the story. When we say, "I want to be a part of what God has done, is doing, and shall do," then the Bible becomes Living Bread, Living Water, and we are swept up in the stream of God's love and power Jesus called the kingdom of God. *That is the power of Scriptures we call authority; it brings us into encounter with the living God.* Through it He compels us to enter the drama of His redemptive purpose in the world. Through Holy Scriptures God makes a covenant with you, and His Story becomes your story and your story becomes His.

If that is the character of the Bible, then we cannot, must not, ignore the Story when we seek to tell its truth. Indeed, its truth is bound up in the Story.

Preaching, Therefore, at Its Core Is the Telling of the Gospel Story

More than the arguing of a line of logic or the elucidation of a set of points to remember, the sermon is the telling of the gospel story. Its purpose then is more than to convince or to inform, but rather to recreate the biblical world in which God creates, redeems, corrects, sets right, loves, and reconciles us to himself. Its primary purpose is to tell the gospel story of God's saving activity —from creation's dawn, to its moment of truth in the Christ event, to its unfolding in history unto this hour and on to the final consummation.

Edmund Steimle, one of my early homiletics professors, pounded away on my overly moralized, overexplained sermons. "Let the story tell itself," he would say. "Have confidence in the story to speak." I have since learned how right he was. To dispense quickly with the story in order to get to the "points" you want to make displays a lack of faith in the Bible to create its own hearers and work its own power.

George Arthur Buttrick, one of the premier preacher-theologians of our century and my teacher in his last few years, taught and demonstrated that the gospel should not be argued, but rather told in vividness and truth. Few, if any, are argued into the faith. Rather, we are invited in, lured, and welcomed by the power, truth, and love of the gospel story. We are swayed not so much by logic as by images, pictures, and stories. The best sermons, then, do not argue propositions or teach "points"; instead, they take us on a journey, a journey along which we meet God and His Christ.[11]

In my own preaching I have found that sermons which retell the Bible stories have far greater power and reach than I could have imagined. Once a woman came to me after a sermon on Moses during which I had told of the Sinai encounter and simply recited the Ten Commandments. She said that when she came into worship her life had felt fragmented and hopeless, but when she heard the simple recital of the Commandments one by one, an unexpected sense of hope surged through her. Another time a young man heard my sermon on Noah; and when he saw how one man had changed the course of history he was filled with excitement and challenge over what one human being can do.

And I as a pastor have found that when I am in one of those dry and barren stretches in my preaching (do we not all suffer them?), the best recipe for renewal is to take one of the Bible stories and retell it in all its vividness and power. It renews my sense of confidence in the power of the Biblical Story to change lives, even the life of the preacher. A rabbi was once asked how to tell a story. He replied:

> A story ... must be told in such a way that it constitutes help in itself.... My grandfather was lame. Once they asked him to tell a story about his teacher. And he related how the holy Baal Shem used to hop and dance while he prayed. My grandfather rose as he spoke, and he was so swept away by his story that he himself began to hop and dance to show how the master had done. From that hour on he was cured of his lameness. That's the way to tell a story![12]

The preacher tells the story of Christ so that as he tells it he will by the grace of God be "changed into his likeness from one degree of glory to another" (2 Cor. 3:18) and be healed.

For these reasons and more that are beyond our understanding we should preach narratively. Doing so fits the nature of God, humankind, Scripture, and the kind of redemption God works in history.

Before we proceed to the how of narrative preaching, I want to develop a model for biblical preaching which I call "the Re-Creation of the Biblical World."

Toward a Model for Preaching:
The Re-Creation of the Biblical World

The preacher's task is first not to re-create the preacher's world or to re-create the hearers' world, but instead to re-create a third

The Theology of Narrative Preaching

reality beyond the preacher and the hearer which I call here "the biblical world." This model should take precedence over a preacher-directed model or a hearer-directed model.

Picture yourself going into a public restaurant alone. You will be dominated by one of two human feelings: the sense of looking at people in the room or of being looked at by those people. Just so, there are two popular models of preaching: 1) the preacher-directed model in which the dominant experience is of looking at the preacher; and 2) the hearer-directed model in which the dominant experience is of being looked at by the preacher. Let us examine each.

MODEL 1: PREACHER DIRECTED

This first model has the presupposition that the congregation learns best from the person of the preacher—the reality of his life, experience, piety, and so forth. It argues that all theology is in part autobiography. Experience is a profound matrix of revelation, God speaking His power and grace into our lives. Testimony then gives us hope that God is indeed active in our lives. Good preaching will not deny experience as a means of knowing the gospel and testimony as a means of sharing it.

This model is based on the assumption that if the preacher can communicate the truth found in his own life, then the sermon will touch corresponding truth in the hearer.

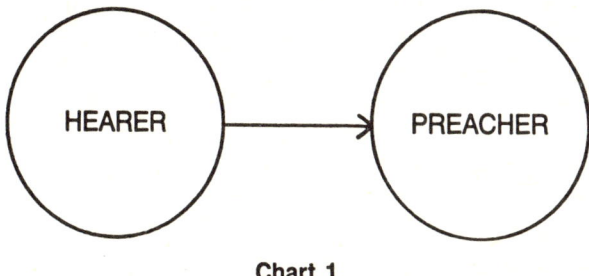

Chart 1

See chart 1 for a diagram of this model. The energy is flowing to the preacher. The dominant experience is of looking at the preacher.

One form of this model, perhaps the best and most compelling, is "confessional preaching." John R. Claypool, my friend and gifted predecessor at Crescent Hill Baptist Church, dramatized the power of what he called "confessional preaching." During the turbulent 1960s he helped keep a generation of Southern Baptist theological students in the pulpit ministry through the power of his preaching. While he consistently preached biblical sermons based on specific texts, he is best known for the "confessional preaching" he did during the long bout with leukemia and death of his daughter, Laura Lou. In his important and profoundly moving book of these "confessional" sermons, *Tracks of a Fellow Struggler,* he spoke of his agonized spiritual journey through her extended illness and death. One sentence captures the essence of "confessional preaching": "See me this morning as your burdened and broken brother, limping back into the family circle to tell you something of what I learned out there in the darkness."[13]

At certain moments in a preacher's life with a church, *not* to preach confessional sermons would be an act of unfaithfulness. John Claypool has introduced the power and importance of such preaching. As a subcategory of the preacher-directed model, however, it shares its shortcomings if practiced as a predominant mode of preaching. (John Claypool and I have corresponded and conversed about the strengths and weaknesses of confessional preaching. He is most aware of the dangers and has responded to these kinds of questions through correspondence and essay.)[14]

If assumed to be a comprehensive model, the preacher-directed model overestimates the depth and the scope of a preacher's life story. In his splendid Beecher lectures, *The Preaching Event,* Claypool wrote an *apologia* for confessional preaching: "Only that which has happened to us can happen through us. . . . The only thing we have to share ultimately is our experience."[15]

There are levels to that comment which are true. This was what Phillips Brooks was getting at in his famous Beecher lectures (1877) when he said that the preacher is not only messenger but also *witness.*[16] Perhaps the most effective sermons we preach are the ones which arise out of our religious experiencing. However, as a dominant model for preaching, preacher-directed preaching

The Theology of Narrative Preaching

is insufficient. Our experience can become a window open to the kingdom of God. But there is far more that can happen in the preaching event than that which has happened to the preacher.

Another shortcoming is that it offers an overidentification of the hearer with the preacher—even when this is not the preacher's intention. A catharsis may take place, but it is the wrong catharsis of the hearer with preacher. Can the hearer see beyond the personality of the preacher to the person of Christ? "For what we preach," said the apostle Paul, "is not ourselves, but Jesus Christ as Lord" (2 Cor. 4:5).

The preacher is the messenger of a deeper reality than an unveiling of the person of the preacher. George Buttrick said in one private conversation: "Jesus Christ is more real to me than I am to myself." That came across in his preaching, where the gospel of Christ was always front and center.

The issue then arises as to the private devotional life of the preacher. If self-knowledge is the primary goal of our devotional life, whether through therapy, meditation, philosophy, or other means, then the sermons are more than likely to become an unveiling of the self. If knowledge of Jesus Christ and deepened relationship with God in Christ is the goal, then the sermons have a better chance of revealing the Christ.

But such a position is not to despise self-knowledge. It is to recognize the limits of self-knowledge.[17] "We are more human than anything else," Harry Stack Sullivan used to say, and that applies to preachers, too. Healthy self-knowledge is invaluable for the preacher. It prevents the preacher from turning the sermon into a self-help kit for his or her own neuroses. It helps defuse hidden agenda that could parade before the people in God-talk. And self-knowledge can lead to deepening relationship of the self with the Self of God. But self-knowledge in and of itself is neither the primary goal of the preacher's spirituality nor the primary focus of his preaching.

Model 1 has two prominent variations. The first is the preacher as hero. The older style of such preaching is filled with examples of the preacher as hero, exemplar of the faith, spiritual giant, effective "soul winner," or counseling genius. So Ernest Campbell well reminds us that the preacher should never make himself the hero of a story in the sermon.

A newer heresy is the preacher as goat. The preacher agonizes publicly over frailty, doubt, anger, lack of piety, or unconventionality in religion. In John Updike's novel of a fallen minister, *A Month of Sundays*, the minister, now spending some time in a psychiatric hospital for some rest and relaxation, recalls such kind of preaching:

> O, shame upon me as I recall those Sundays in the world, my sermons so fetchingly agonized, so fashionably antinomian. I suffered, impaled upon those impossible texts . . . pale in my pantomime of holy agitation, self-pleasing in my sleepless sweat, a fevered scapegoat taking upon myself the sins of the prosperous.[18]

Many modern preachers might use Henri Nouwen's profound image of the "wounded healer" as a justification for unveiling one's sins before the people, but Nouwen himself warns:

> On the one hand, no minister can keep his own experience of life hidden from those he wants to help. . . . On the other hand, it would be very easy to misuse the concept of the wounded healer by defending a form of spiritual exhibitionism. A minister who talks in the pulpit about his own personal problems is of no help to his congregation, for no suffering human being is helped by someone who tells him that he has the same problems.[19]

In both cases, preacher as hero or preacher as goat, the focus of the sermons is on the preacher, whether exemplar of the faith or chief of all sinners. There are times when sermons are properly preacher centered, when confessional preaching is a powerful vehicle for encounter with the living God. But as a dominant model it is insufficient.

Model 2: Hearer Centered

In this second model of preaching, the dominant sense of the congregation is of being looked at by the preacher. The hearer feels very much known by and addressed by the preacher. See chart 2 for the illustration of this model.

The Theology of Narrative Preaching

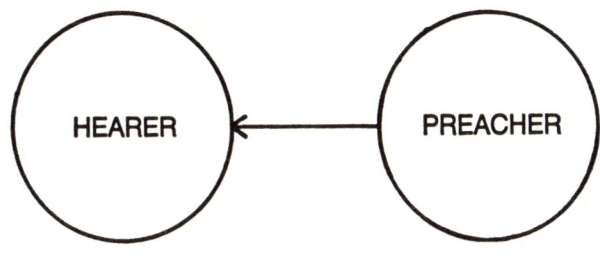

Chart 2

The energy is flowing from preacher to hearer. The preacher in such a model may be variously Angry Father or Sensitive Pastor.

In the Angry Father variation of model 2 the preacher assumes the pose of angry, judging father, and the hearers feel riveted to the back of the pew with the message: you sinner, you need to be more committed, etc. Many a Christian limps into church Sunday after Sunday seeking the good news of Jesus Christ only to hear the condemnation of a preacher acting as angry father. These sermons are not only accusatory in tone, but they also are largely imperative in mode: "You ought" is the major appeal.

In the second variation the preacher is Sensitive Pastor preaching "Life-Situation" sermons. The preacher addresses the urgent, crying, personal needs of the person in the pew. The counseling and crisis ministry of the church becomes seedbed for sermons. This approach is tender and pastoral in tone. The people feel intimately known and intensely addressed by the preacher.

Perhaps the most compelling practitioner of Life-Situation preaching in our century is Harry Emerson Fosdick. In his struggle to find a meaningful form of communicating the gospel and in his frustration with the deadness of the old-style expository preaching ("Only the preacher," he wrote, "proceeds still upon the idea that folk come to church desperately anxious to discover what happened to the Jebusites"), Fosdick discovered the power of Life-Situation preaching. He would begin with a deeply felt need of the people, examine various solutions, and then supply the biblical answer.[20]

Such Life-Situation preaching is an important mode of preaching, and, as in Confessional Preaching, there are times when not to preach directly to the needs of the people would be an act of pastoral unfaithfulness. The teachable moment comes as it comes, not according to our calendars, so there are significant moments when Life-Situation preaching is demanded. However, as a dominant model for preaching, the hearer-directed model even at its best is insufficient.

There are four shortcomings of Model 2. The first is that it ignores the initiative of God's Word. If the pulpit is only responsive to the expressed needs of the people, it does not leave room for a disciplined diet of the Word of God to speak its word to the people, setting priorities, defining true needs, creating its hearers, and answering the proper questions rather than the ones we think are most important. The expressed needs of the people may not be their deepest needs.

The second danger, then, of this kind of preaching is that it presumes that the congregation knows their deepest needs or that the needs they "feel" are their deepest needs. As human beings we are infinitely self-deceptive; we are easily distracted by penultimate needs and so neglect our ultimate needs. Esau traded his blessing for porridge. Sermons may dispense porridge instead of the blessing of God.[21] Life-Situation preaching shares a theological weakness with Paul Tillich's method of correlation whereby the world asks the question and the church supplies the biblical answer. Sometimes, many times, the world does not ask the right questions. Rarely in Jesus' ministry did he answer a question directly. Most often he heard the question, restated it, and then answered the corrected question.

The third danger is that it presumes that the preacher knows the needs of the people when in fact the pastor may only have his finger on the pulse of a few people, or worse, only on his own pulse.

The fourth danger is that the communication may be too direct to be effective. When a person feels too directly addressed, especially if there is some confrontation involved, then that person tends to duck for cover or dodge the words as they come. We must take into consideration that communication can be too direct, too fresh, too intensely personal for maximum effectiveness. As the poet Auden wrote: "Truth, like love and sleep, resents/Approaches that are too intense."[22]

MODEL 3: RE-CREATING THE BIBLICAL WORLD

There is a third way I would propose to be a better comprehensive model for preaching. The preacher points to a third reality beyond the preacher's world and the hearer's world: the reality of the biblical world.

The Bible calls us to enter a new world even as we live in this old one, to strike a covenant, to make God's Story our story, and to enter the Kingdom of God. It invites us to a new way of seeing, knowing, and behaving.

Model 3 seeks to create, or re-create, a third reality in the worship event of the community: the unfolding of the biblical world. See chart 3 for the illustration of Model 3.

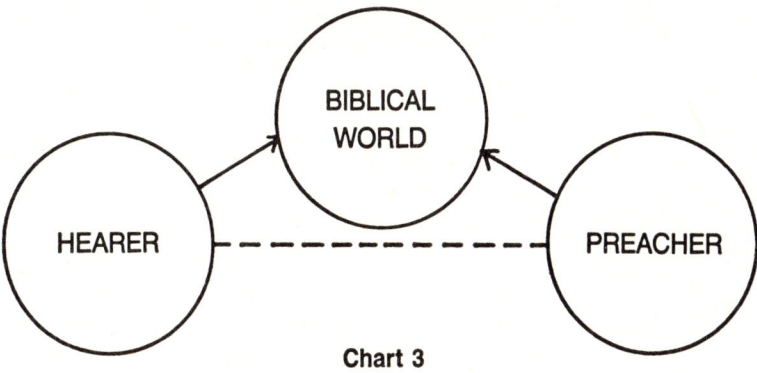

Chart 3

Note that I have drawn a dotted line between the preacher and the hearer because preaching is always a form of personal communication. One cannot improve upon Phillips Brooks's famous definition of preaching as "communication of truth by man to men . . . the bringing of truth through personality."[23] But note that he did not say that it is the communication of *personality* through personality. He was making the eloquent point that in real preaching the gospel travels *through* the whole person of the preacher to the congregation, not *over* that person to the congregation.[24]

Now to the new dominant circle added to the diagram, the biblical world.

The Biblical World

The biblical world is the sphere of life in which God is active. Life in the biblical world is the combination of the presence and activity of God on the one hand and the faith and obedience of God's people on the other. In the biblical world God speaks, to use Buechner's image, an alphabet of grace which, like the Hebrew alphabet, has only consonants. God speaks and acts the consonants and we, His people, fill in the vowels with "all the faith and imagination we can muster."[25] In the biblical world, all history is faith history (so history and story are one) and all revelation is a divine-human enterprise—like the mutuality of a dance.

The biblical world is the world of history and meaning in which God is active in His creative, "righteousing" and reconciling power. For people of faith the biblical world is a way of experiencing reality in the truest and fullest possible way. And why not? The author of reality has created it. The biblical world has been passed down "from faith to faith." It is a world told by the voice of faith, heard by the ears of faith, seen by the eyes of faith, and lived in "the obedience of faith" (Rom. 1:5). Faith is how we enter the biblical world. And as we enter we experience adoption as God's child, we gain the vocation of justice, peace, and love in society, we receive forgiveness and healing, and we are made whole by the grace of Jesus Christ in us. From within that world we experience and live life differently—and more fully, for the biblical world is truer than the world of *Playboy,* than the world of Madison Avenue, than Yuppie World, Pentagon World, or TV World.

The biblical world is a world of creation and fall, of justice and hope, of rebellion and tragedy, of welcome and grace, of faith and freedom, of invitation and decision, of conflict and consummation.[26] It is a world begun by the creating God, sustained by a strong God, preserved by an infinitely patient God, and redeemed by a God whose love will not let us go.

When we enter this biblical world we discover that we live life better and truer from inside it. We do not just understand life better, but we are given grace's pardon and power with which to live life "more abundantly." When we enter the biblical story we have a saving relationship with God and are enlisted to carry His saving power to the world, to be a light to the nations, salt to the earth.

As an image of the biblical world take the magnificent Cathedral of Chartres in France. As you walk into its doors, you enter the "many-storied" universe of the biblical world. In its stained glass and sculpture the cathedral tells the Story and the stories. The Gothic ediface is but the binding of the one great book of life whose text is found in the windows and sculpture. The cathedral was the church, the library, the university, and the meeting house of the medieval town; but, most importantly of all, the cathedral re-created the Biblical Story in its many-storied universe. It was a scholar's paradise, but it was also the people's book for those who could neither read nor write.

The many-storied universe of the cathedral begins with creation. It tells of the fall, of Old Testament heroes and heroines, and of New Testament figures of faith. It pictures prophecy fulfilled with the coming of Jesus. The four New Testament evangelists sit on the shoulders of the Old Testament prophets. All the great stories of the Bible are told, on to the last judgment and the glorious new heaven and new earth bejeweled with cut glass and sunlight in the south rose window. To walk through the cathedral is to walk back and forth through time; it is to live in the conviction of the divine plan and purpose; it is to have a past, present, and future rich beyond measure.

Preaching, good preaching, re-creates such a many-storied universe. It points to the biblical world. It tells the Biblical Story. What could be more crucial than that?

Re-Creating the Biblical World

The preacher's task is to create a third reality beyond the worlds of the preacher and hearer: the biblical world. The major focus is on God and His way with us in the world as revealed in Scripture and in Jesus of Nazareth.

The biblical world, however, is not a distant third world unconnected with the world of the preacher and the hearer. So in chart

4 you see arrows going in both directions from hearer to biblical world as well as from biblical world to hearer, from the preacher to the biblical world and back.

A biblical world unconnected to the preacher's or hearer's world becomes a relic of the past or a fortress of impossible holiness. Many preachers in the name of "preaching the Bible" make of the Bible a museum ("what happened to the Jebusites?") or they turn the biblical world into an unreal stained glass universe uninhabitable except by ancient or modern saints. Such Biblicism does not draw the kingdom nigh but rather distances the biblical world from an admiring or incredulous (as the case may be) hearer.

Retelling the Biblical Story involves, therefore, "a shared story." As Rice and Niedenthal develop, the preacher tells a "shared story" which combines the Biblical Story, the preacher's story, the hearer's story, and the church's story (both local congregation and church universal).[27] So we might add a circle to our illustration:

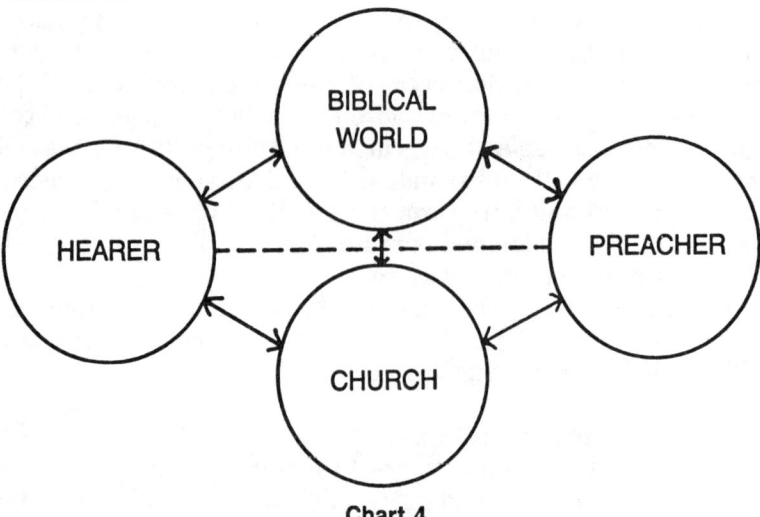

Chart 4

While the biblical world always remains central, it draws into itself the worlds, or stories, of the preacher, hearer, and church. The more the preacher can show the biblical world to be filled with images from our world, the more real and inviting that world will become. Good sermons evoke the deepest experiences, hopes, and dreams of the people. It shows that the kingdom of God *is,* as Jesus said, among us. Therefore, good preaching draws upon the preacher's world and is always to some degree "confessional"; it draws upon the hearer's world and is always "life-situational"; it draws upon the church's world and is inescapably ecclesiastical; but its primary point of reference is the biblical world. For the biblical world is the true world, God's world in which we "live and move and have our being."

The preacher re-creates the biblical world because this is the only healing, saving world in which to live. This biblical world has created us and called us and even now empowers us. Preaching keeps this world vivid and accessible to the people of God.

There is another reason why the re-creation of a third world is important. It is good communication. Communication can, as I suggested above, be too direct for its own good. The preacher can be too fresh and assume too much intimacy. "Eyeball-to-eyeball" is not always the most effective communication.

Therefore, the telling of a story, the re-creation of a Third World, creates enough personal distance so that the message can be heard. It is sometimes easier to "overhear" than to "hear"—especially when we speak of life and death. This point has been eloquently made by Fred Craddock in his Beecher Lectures, *Overhearing the Gospel.*[28] Using Kierkegaard's thought, he demonstrates that things we know too well are best heard indirectly, as through parables and stories.

Model 3 points not to the preacher or to the hearer, but to a third reality, the biblical world, and so offers creative distance. Perhaps this way we can experience the gospel story as it was meant to be—as gracious invitation. The preacher points to the biblical world in the hope and faith that it will create its own hearers and draw these hearers into itself.

In Karl Barth's study there hung a print of Grünewald's crucifixion. In the center of the painting is the crucified Christ. Off to the right is the stark figure of John the Baptist pointing his almost too long index finger to the Christ. That is the posture of preaching. The preacher points; the preacher points not to himself, nor at the hearer, nor to the church, but toward the Christ. The preacher tells the gospel story and re-creates the biblical world of God's saving activity and our response of "wonder, love, and praise."

The biblical world has wonderful stories to tell. They are mysterious, outrageous, and comic; they are sad, scary, and glad. They make us laugh and cry; they cause our spines to tingle and hair to stand on the back of our necks. They call us to enter them in faith and obedience.

Listen to them. As you do, may God draw you into Himself.

The How of Narrative Preaching

We have tried to state the why of narrative preaching. Now let us move more practically to the how of it.

How do we retell the Bible stories? We do not merely memorize the text and regurgitate it verbatim. Somehow the "old, old story" must come alive as it merges with our life stories. So first we must consider the role of the preacher.

THE PREACHER AS STORYTELLER

The preacher is the storyteller and as such must consider the sacred role of the narrator. The narrator provides distance on the story so that we can step back a bit and look at it. This distance allows the story to become a "shared story." The preacher lets his story, the hearer's story, the congregation's (and the church's) story enter the Biblical Story and become part of it.

As you let the Biblical Story speak to you, allow it to enter your world and the worlds of your hearers. Listen deeply not only to the Biblical Story, but also to your own life and the life of your people. Invite the Holy Spirit to open the deep resonances of the Biblical Story in your life story and the life stories of your people. The narrator-preacher tells the Biblical Story in such a way that it becomes a shared story. When this happens, the hearers are invited in.

The preacher as storyteller tells the Story so that our stories are part of it.

1. *Trusting the Story.*—We must trust the Biblical Story to carry its own power. This is a matter of faith, of spiritual posture. Do

The Theology of Narrative Preaching

we stand over the text as judges, or do we let the text judge us? What is truer, the Biblical Story or our stories? Paul Minear was once reported to have told Rudolf Bultmann, "Dr. Bultmann, the difference between us is that you think that we should de-mythologize the New Testament. I think the New Testament should de-mythologize us!"[29]

Do we stand in awe under the mystery of God as we hear the Bible stories? In narrative preaching we begin in awe as we stand under the power of the Bible narrative. Narrative preaching begins in wonder.

As we retell the biblical stories, we seek to create what Paul Ricoeur suggestively calls "a second naivete."[30] It is the spiritual simplicity beyond complexity. We dispense with all our modern questions long enough to give ourselves over, in the wager of faith, to the truth of the narrative. We may not listen to the Bible stories with the first naivete of a child (that would be a false naivete); but unless we become as children and listen to the Bible stories with a second naivete, we may never meet the God who first spoke them and moves in the midst of them.

The gamble of faith says: I will trust that the truth of the biblical narrative world is truer than any other world I can live in; its vision is truer than any other vision of the world available, including my own. It says: I will enter the Story and follow the God who created it in hope that in the following I will meet that God and live life more abundantly.

Good narrative preaching re-creates the biblical world and evokes a "second naivete" so that the congregation will be moved to enter it. The preacher here is the storyteller who spins the story in all its indicative matter-of-factness. The preacher does not dissect the story surgeonlike and debate its details. He does not explain it; he tells it. If the preacher spends his sermon time rehearsing the historical-critical debates about the text, he will distance the hearers from the story. If, however, he re-creates the story as the real world of God, he will invite participation in the story. Here are two examples in the sermons that precede: in the Noah sermon I do not question how God could have sent the flood, I re-present it as the uncreating of the world, the undoing of the third day of creation; in the Jacob sermon I do not try to explain the wrestling at the Jabbok river; I retell it in all its primal mystery and awe.

Undoubtedly some people hear these sermons in a first naiveté rather than a second naiveté. I would call the second naiveté a postcritical (not anticritical) religious awareness. Children in the congregation will hear these sermons in their natural first naiveté; fine, this will serve to stimulate their religious imagination. Some adults will hear them in an anticritical first naiveté. Others will defend themselves against the power of the story with their carefully honed critical tools. (Surely you don't believe that! That is a late Bronze Age world view.) Narrative preaching, however, takes the risk of allowing the story to be heard on different levels, in the hope that in the long run this kind of preaching will discourage the congregation from debating things *about* the story and, instead, invite them to enter it.

2. *Keeping the Story Primary.*—Trusting in the Biblical Story also means we let it remain primary in the sermon structure itself. The story itself will dominate the sermon. We will not strain to make "points."

Once I saw a preacher don biblical costume and do a first-person monologue sermon as a biblical character. It was excellent. But too soon he pulled off his robe and beard, became himself, and preached a three-point sermon on the monologue, saying, in effect, "Now this is what I was trying to tell you in the story." It ruined the preaching event. Too many sermons are like that. Instead, allow the story to be the shape of the entire sermon. Trust it. Tell it.

In Marie L. Shedlock's classic *The Art of the Story-Teller,* she warns against those stories where the moral detaches itself and explains the story.[31] In *Alice in Wonderland* the Duchess says, "And the moral of *that* is: Take care of the sense and the sounds will take care of themselves." Alice says to herself, "How fond she is of finding morals." It is weary business for the child and the child in all of us to hear someone belabor the moral of the story. Shedlock, a master storyteller herself, says:

> Pointing out the moral of the story has always seemed as futile as tying a flower onto a stalk instead of letting the flower grow

out of the stalk, as Nature intended. In the first case, the flower, showy and bright for a moment, soon fades away. In the second instance, it develops slowly, coming to perfection in fulness of time because of the life within.[32]

Should we not have that much confidence in the Word of God to plant the seed and let God bring it to harvest in His good time? The seed grows secretly, Jesus said, while we wake and even while we sleep.

Whatever "points" or "morals" you want to get across, let them arise from the story as the story unfolds. Do not divide the sermon into story time and application time. Teach the morals through the action of the story as the story goes along. The great Bible stories do not so much *have* morals as they *are* morals. They enflesh the righteousness of God.

The Tools of Narrative Preaching

The preacher should make the best use of the tools of good storytelling: action, irony, pace, mood, character development, and so on. Some important techniques are these:

1. *Visualization.*—A picture is worth a thousand words. Help the listeners picture what's going on. Picture the rich man in Jesus' parable of the rich man and Lazarus: he is not just eating a lavish meal; picture him eating roast duckling with orange sauce.

2. *Anachronism.*—Anachronism is the use of details which are chronologically out of place in order to convey the meaning vividly. Picture the rich man in a tuxedo. Or you may tell an entire scene in a modern idiom. A contemporary master of anachronism is Frederick Buechner. See especially his ABC of biblical characters, *Peculiar Treasures.*[33]

Anachronism may be bold, even outrageous; but be sure it *serves* the story instead of distracting from it.

3. *Biblical Scholarship.*—The contemporary preacher can make good use of biblical scholarship. Biblical scholarship helps us discover important clues to the meaning of the narrative. It gives us clues to the plot, the characters, the mood, and the meaning. The new literary criticism movement in biblical studies

which focuses on the final form of the text is especially helpful. An excellent beginning point would be Alan Culpepper's *Anatomy of the Fourth Gospel*.[34]

Biblical scholarship also helps us close the enormous cultural gap between the biblical times and ours. It helps us determine what the biblical passage first meant to its first tellers and hearers, a necessity for good and honest preaching.

Biblical scholarship also helps us explore the different facets of the narrative. A Bible story may be approached from several different directions. Understanding this may help you make proper choices as to what to leave in or out or what to emphasize.

Biblical scholarship also helps us recognize the important theological themes and to relate these to overarching theological themes in the Bible. Such was the strength of the biblical theology movement in our century.

I add two words of warning. The tools of biblical criticism are best *invisible* tools in the sermon itself. Keep your technical scholarship in the study. To parade your scholarship before the people is at best tiresome and at worst pretentious, and it almost always deflects attention from the story.

Also, if the story has something in it that is so foreign to our culture that you will have to explain it carefully and extensively in order for it to make sense, you have a choice to make. In most cases an historical detail in a story is like a joke; if you have to explain it, it ruins the story. If the obscure detail is not important to the story it may best be left out. If it is crucial, for example, as the rules of levirate marriage in Ruth are crucial for understanding Ruth, then you must exercise your role as the storyteller boldly. Step in, tell the audience that you must explain something, do it concisely and clearly, and then move on.

In general the advice of Marie Shedlock is to be heeded: do not overexplain details in the story or use too many extraneous details. She quotes this passage from *Don Quixote* with good effect: Sancho Panza is trying to tell Don Quixote a story.

> "In a village of Estramadura there was a shepherd—no I mean a goatherd—which shepherd or goatherd as my story says, was called Lope Ruiz—and this Lope Ruiz was in love with a shep-

herdess called Torralva, who was daughter to a rich herdsman, and this rich herdsman—"

"If this be thy story, Sancho," said Don Quixote, "thou wilt not have done these two days. Tell it concisely, like a man of sense, or else say no more."[35]

The story is told of a mother reading Bible stories to her child and skipping one because it was too difficult for her child to understand. The little voice protested: "I can understand them all perfectly well, if only you wouldn't explain them to me."[36]

4. *The Use of Typology.*—In narrative preaching typology is possible again.[37]

Typology was one of the ways the people of God have tried to unite the Old and New Testaments (along with prophecy and allegory). Typology seeks out and speaks the correspondences and patterns in the ways God has revealed Himself through persons and events. Typology was used in the New Testament itself: "As Jonah was three days and three nights in the belly of the whale, so will the Son of man be three days and three nights in the heart of the earth" (Matt. 12:40); or, "As Moses lifted up the serpent in the wilderness, so must the Son of man be lifted up" (John 3:14).

Typology discovers and expresses patterns of God's activity all through salvation history. So Jesus is pictured in Matthew as the new Moses, giving His new law in the Sermon on the Mount and delivering us as Moses delivered God's people from Pharaoh.

The history of the use of typology is an interesting one. It has been used and misused and has fallen in and out of favor.[38] In the Middle Ages typology (then in favor) was systemized. For example, in the *Biblia Pauperum,* triple sectioned woodcuts featured the New Testament scene in the middle and Old Testament types on each side. For example, Jesus' descent into the tomb is flanked by Joseph's descent into the well and Jonah's into the whale.[39]

Modern biblical criticism has called into question the use of typology, and many modern preachers are timid to use it. But we would listen well to New Testament scholar Reginald Fuller, who says: "Typology is based upon the conviction that God acts consistently in history, that his actions conform to a pattern because he is what he is. Hence his final redemption will conform to the pattern of the preliminary redemption in the Exodus."[40]

Narrative theology makes typology possible again because it believes there is an author who has written the entire story so there may be types, correspondences, and patterns that even the particular authors of and characters in the biblical stories did not see. In fact, typology may be the most appropriate form of exposition of the narrative of the Bible. The literary critic Northrup Frye asserts boldly that: "This typological way of reading the Bible is indicated too often and explicitly in the N.T. itself for us to be in any doubt that this is the 'right' way of reading it."[41]

Frye joins Fuller in his estimation of typology: "What typology is as a mode of thought, what it both assumes and leads to is a theory of history, or more accurately of historical process: an assumption that there is some meaning and point to history and that sooner or later some event or events will occur which will indicate what that meaning or point is, and so become an antitype of what has happened previously."[42]

Our use of typology in narrative preaching is based on a staggering assumption: The same God who created the world is at work in both Testaments and all history. All activity of God, therefore, will have correspondences, patterns, or types. That history of God proceeds even to our day as the life of the church becomes "the Third Testament." Our modern lives, also, then find correspondences in the biblical events and persons. God has not changed his character or purpose; neither has our basic character changed. Therefore, we can truly be brother and sister to the characters in the Biblical Story; they are *us*. So typology not only explains the Bible; it also illumines our existence.

A word of caution: Our use of typology can easily become fanciful and false. To keep us honest, therefore, typology must have guidelines: (1) We must first take seriously the original historical meaning of the event or character; this original meaning must not be cast aside; and (2) When the original meaning is guaranteed, then the typological (larger, deeper, extended) meaning must make a real connection in meaning with the original. For example, the typological coupling of the divine rescue of the children of Israel through the Red Sea and the waters of Christian baptism is proper since both are "rescue" events. But to match the Nile turning to blood with Jesus turning water into wine at Cana, just because in both cases the water turned red, is not proper.[43]

In narrative preaching typology is possible because it conveys all history as one fabric—the creating, protecting, and redeeming activity of God. Creation, fall, Old Testament, New Testament, and history to the present are one divine-human story. In such a drama of redemption the imagination of the preacher can be used to discern and depict correspondence of image, event, and person and so tell of God's salvation-history with power.

Another assumption of Christian narrative preaching is its Christocentric focus. The very word of God that brought creation, history, and the people of God into being and made all reality the plot of His providential care and redeeming love was made flesh and came to dwell with us in Jesus of Nazareth. So. . . .

Jesus Christ as God's Favorite Story

Jesus Christ is the center and circumference of the Biblical Story.

Flannery O'Connor says that there are three ways to write a novel: (1) Start at the beginning and write to the end; (2) Start at the end and write backward to the start; or (3) Start at the crucial event of the story and then write backward to the beginning and forward to the end.

The Christian says that God's Story reaches its crucial moment in Jesus the Christ. From the perspective of His life, death, and resurrection, we see history all the way back to its beginning and forward to its culmination. So all history and all Scriptures point to Christ. Therefore, in narrative preaching it is important to keep the heart of the story, the gospel of God in Christ, in its horizon. Jesus Christ shows us truest of all what God is up to in the world. All stories therefore find their hidden or open meaning in him. After all, as Colossians and the Gospel of John affirm, the One made flesh in Jesus was God's favorite story from the beginning, the one in whom, through whom, and for whom all creation is made and every story is told.

Rediscovering Jewish Roots: Narrative Preaching as Christian *Hagadah*

Narrative preaching is in one sense a rediscovery of our Jewish roots. It was no accident that when Jesus came preaching He told parables. If philosophy is the genius of the Greek mind, storytelling is the genius of the Hebrew mind, and we Christian preachers tend to be more Greek than Hebrew. It was the brilliant Jewish storyteller Elie Wiesel whose retelling of Old Testament stories fired my imagination to attempt these kinds of sermons; you will see my debt to him.

Narrative preaching is Christian *hagadah*. Let me explain. The ancient rabbinic commentary on Scripture consisted of two kinds: (1) *halakah*, which was the exposition of the Law into rules for daily living; and (2) *hagadah*, which was the use of storytelling to communicate the revelation of God. Sometimes *hagadah* retold the biblical stories, other times new stories, and sometimes the old and the new merged. The great rabbinic scholar C. G. Montefiore says that *halakah* was the rabbis' most ardent pursuit, but, "Hagadah was their relaxation and amusement; in Hagadah their fancy and imagination found its occupation."[44]

Hagadah is full of passion, poignance, laughter, and sadness. God is often pictured in outrageously human form but only because the rabbis so reverenced Him. Old Testament characters were flesh and blood people. Sometimes they were made to jump time and space and talk with one another. Montefiore rightly speaks of the freedom and exaggeration of *hagadah*, of its absurdities and its excellences.[45]

Christian *hagadah* is the retelling of the great story of redemption which centers in Christ and reaches back to creation and onward to consummation. Early Christian *kerygma* was *hagadah*. C. H. Dodd has summarized it:

(1) The prophecies are fulfilled, and the New Age is inaugurated by the coming of Christ.
(2) He was born of the seed of David.
(3) He died according to the Scriptures, to deliver us out of this present evil age.
(4) He was buried.

(5) He rose on the third day according to the Scriptures.
(6) He is exalted at the right hand of God, as the Son of God and Lord of the quick and the dead.
(7) He will come again as judge and Saviour of men.[46]

What early Christian preaching did (and what our narrative preaching does) was to proclaim the *kerygma* and to stretch it back to creation (Col. 1:15-20) and on to the end (Rev. 21). It is our call to keep the Story alive.

Christian *hagadah* is not the only kind of preaching. Today's Christians need *halakah* too.[47] We need ethics along with story. We need the Ten Commandments along with the Exodus and the Sermon on the Mount along with the parables.[48] Let us not, however, so concentrate on teaching moral precepts or philosophical truths that we forget *hagadah,* the Great Story and stories from whence our faith and life have been hewn. Let us tell the Story with all the freedom, passion, and truth which God gives us in his holy book and through the holy imagination of His Spirit.

Notes

1. The statement of purpose in preaching varies widely. Is it to convince the hearer of the truth of the gospel (John A. Broadus, *A Treatise on the Preparation and Delivery of Sermons*)? Is it to dispense information about the Bible or about theology (for example, didactic preaching among fundamentalists)? Is it to motivate hearers to do certain things? Is it to effect a reconciliation with God (Claypool, *The Preaching Event*)? Is not the foundation of all these to provide a meeting place for us with God? Or to meet Christ, as James Stewart puts it (*Heralds of God*)?

2. John Shea, *Stories of God: An Unauthorized Biography* (Chicago: The Thomas More Press, 1978), p. 8.

3. Alfred North Whitehead, *Process and Reality* (New York: The Macmillan Co., 1929), p. 526.

4. Steven Crites, "The Narrative Quality of Experience," *Journal of the American Academy of Religion,* 39 (September 1971), 291-311, argues the essential dimension of having a history, or living in the "tensed unity" of past, present, and future, as distinctive of the human consciousness. Amos Wilder argues in "Story and Story World," *Interpretation,* 37 (October 1983), 359 f., that the urgency and necessity of storytelling

throughout history has been to "place" us in the past, present, and future stream of time, to reduce the "terror of history."

5. Stanley Hauerwas, *A Community of Character* (Notre Dame: University of Notre Dame Press, 1981), pp. 9 ff., 129 ff.

6. Johann Metz, *Faith in History and Society,* trans. David Smith (New York: The Seabury Press, 1980), pp. 205-28. Also, Robert McAfee Brown, "My Story and 'The Story,'" *Theology Today,* 22:166-73. See also James Cone, *The Spirituals and The Blues* (New York: The Seabury Press, 1972).

7. "Some Implications of Narrative Theology for Ministry to Cancer Patients." *Journal of Pastoral Care,* 38 (September 29, 1984), 216-225. Isak Dinesen said, "All sorrows can be borne if you put them into a story or tell a story about them." Quoted in Hannah Arendt, *The Human Condition* (Garden City: Doubleday Anchor Book, 1958), p. 175.

8. In W. Jackson Bate, *Samuel Johnson* (New York: Harcourt Brace Jovanovich, 1975), p. 234.

9. Northrup Frye in *The Great Code* (London: Ark Paperbacks, 1983) argues as a literary critic that the Bible is a "great code" of truth and meaning whose basic form is a poetic narrative. "The primary and literal meaning of the Bible, then is its . . . poetic meaning. It is only when we are reading as we do when we read poetry that we can take the word 'literal' seriously, accepting every word given us without question" (p. 61). He argues that the writing of the Bible "is not primarily . . . a metonymic (philosophical) consistency of doctrine addressed to our faith: it is a unity of narrative and imagery" (p. 62). Frye enumerates the seven stages of biblical narrative, or seven phases of revelation, as: creation, exodus, law, wisdom, prophecy, gospel, and apocalypse.

From a theological perspective the Biblical Theology Movement caught the narrative character of our faith. G. Ernest Wright is a representative spokesperson: "Biblical Theology is first and foremost a theology of recital in which Biblical man confesses his faith by reciting the formative events of his history as the redemptive handiwork of God" (*God Who Acts: Biblical Theology as Recital*—London: SCM Press, 1952, p. 38).

The question then has been persistently raised as to the relationship of story and history. Contemporary scholars are reconsidering the issue. We may not have to choose so severely between the two. Frye argues that the distinction would never have occurred to the biblical writers and that it is an inappropriate question. So he argues (contra Bultmann) that "to demythologize any part of the Bible would be the same thing as to obliterate it" (p. 30).

James Barr would find in Frye a comrade as he criticizes the Biblical Theology Movement for its simplistic identification of biblical narratives with "pure" history. Barr counters, "The long narrative corpus of the O.T. seems to me, as a body of literature, to merit the title of story rather than history," though we may call it with Hans Frei, "history-like." Israel's genius was in its storytelling (James Barr, "Story and History in Biblical Theology" in his *Explorations in Theology,* No. 7—London: SCM Press, 1980, pp. 5,27).

There is a large body of scholars today who would argue that there is no such thing as an unstoried history, that there is no world apart from a language world; and so, not only is it inappropriate to try to separate history and story; it is impossible. Amos Wilder counters by maintaining that while history and story may be inseparable there *is a real* world by which to test the truth of story worlds: "Behind our clouded visions of the world there is a prior sense for the real which continues to test them" ("Story and Story World," *Interpretation,* 37—October 1983, p. 364).

I would agree, and would Culpepper, with Wilder. When people hear the story world of the biblical narrative, they should say, "Yes, this is the world, the truest depiction of all reality, and I live truer, freer, and more abundantly from within it." (See note 32.)

I like Alan Culpepper's phrase describing biblical narrative: "a story of history interpreted by faith" (*Anatomy of the Fourth Gospel*—Philadelphia: Fortress Press, 1983, p. 232). It best captures the narrative of the biblical revelation for biblical revelation is essentially a Divine-human enterprise—God speaking/acting and humankind listening/responding. History and story are inextricably bound. History is by necessity story—it is life lived in the presence of God, seen with the eyes of faith, heard with the ears of faith, and acted upon in the obedience of faith. To try to separate the two is like trying to separate the vowels and consonants of a word. (See note 25 and corresponding text.)

10. See Frederick Buechner's delightful treatment of this episode in his Beecher Lectures, *Telling the Truth: The Gospel as Tragedy, Comedy, and Fairy Tale* (New York: Harper and Row, 1977), p. 49 ff.

11. In *The Homiletical Plot* (Atlanta: John Knox Press, 1980) Eugene Lowry argues similarly that the sermon is at its best a piece of narrative art with a narrative plot, a journey more than an outline. His model narrative plot has five movements: (1) upsetting the equilibrium (Oops); (2) analyzing the discrepancy (Ugh); (3) disclosing the clue to resolution (Aha); (4) experiencing the gospel (Whee); and (5) anticipating the consequences (Yeah). Lowery correctly does not advocate imposing this plot on

all narrative texts, but uses it as the model plot which most good sermons and stories have.

12. Martin Buber, *Tales of the Hasidim* (London: Thames and Hudson, 1956), pp. v-vi.
13. John Claypool, *Tracks of a Fellow Struggler* (Waco: Word Books, 1974), p. 26.
14. John Claypool, "Confessional Preaching" in *Preaching in Today's World*, compiler, James C. Barry (Nashville: Broadman, 1984), p. 62 ff.
15. John Claypool, *The Preaching Event* (Waco: Word Books, 1980), p. 108.
16. Phillips Brooks, *Lectures on Preaching* (London: H. R. Allenson, 1902), p. 14.
17. See Walker Percy's *Lost in the Cosmos: The Last Self-Help Book* (New York: Farrar, Straus & Giroux, 1983) for a delightful and provocative challenge to our age's easy assumptions about self-knowledge and its idolatrous grasping for it.
18. John Updike, *A Month of Sundays* (New York: Alfred A. Knopf, 1965), p. 26.
19. Henri Nouwen, *The Wounded Healer* (New York: Image Books, 1979), p. 88.
20. Harry Emerson Fosdick, *The Living of These Days* (New York: Harper & Row, 1956), p. 92 ff.
21. See Reginald Fuller, *What Is Liturgical Preaching?* (London: SCM Press, 1957), pp. 16-17.
22. W. H. Auden, "New Year Letter" (London: Faber & Faber, 1941), p. 27.
23. Phillips Brooks, *Lectures on Preaching* (London: H. R. Allenson, 1902), p. 5. One of course can improve on the exclusive language. Try "by human persons to human persons."
24. Ibid., p. 8.
25. Frederick Buechner, *The Sacred Journey* (San Francisco: Harper & Row, 1982), p. 4.
26. See Shea, *Stories of God* (Chicago: The Thomas More Press, 1978), for a discussion of themes like these.
27. Edmund Steimle, Morris Niedenthal, Charles L. Rice, *Preaching the Story* (Philadelphia: Fortress Press, 1980), pp. 1-18.
28. Fred B. Craddock, *Overhearing the Gospel: Preaching and Teaching the Faith to Persons Who Have Already Heard* (Nashville: Abingdon, 1978).
29. Reported by J. Louis Martyn, professor of New Testament at Union Theological Seminary, New York City.

30. Paul Ricoeur, *The Symbolism of Evil* (Boston: Beacon Press, 1967), p. 35. Also developed in the last chapter.

31. Marie L. Shedlock, *The Art of the Story-Teller* (New York: Dover, 1951), p. 60.

32. Ibid., pp. 19-20.

33. Frederick Buechner, *Peculiar Treasures* (New York: Harper & Row, 1979).

34. See Alan Culpepper, *Anatomy of the Fourth Gospel* (Philadelphia: Fortress Press, 1983). Professor Culpepper's work is not only a brilliant study of John's Gospel but is a pioneering venture into a new form of literary criticism of the Bible which may help us beyond the debilitating fundamentalist/modernist conflict that never seems to let us go. Culpepper says, "The future role of the gospel in the life of the church will depend on the church's ability to relate both story and history to truth in such a way that neither has an exclusive claim to truth and one is not incompatible with the other. Only then will the distorting blinkers of the contemporary world be set aside so that the gospel can be read as the evangelist assumed it would be" (p. 236). What he calls "narrative world" is close to what I call the biblical world and what Amos Wilder calls "story-world" or "world-plot."

35. Shedlock, *The Art of the Story-Teller* (New York: Dover, 1951), p. 19.

36. Arthur John Gossip, *Experience Worketh Hope* (New York: Charles Scribner's Sons, 1945), p. 77.

37. My argument is that a postcritical narrative theology can resurrect typology (or figuration as Hans Frei calls it) from historical criticism's wastebasket. It was an invaluable tool of precritical realistic or literal reading of Scripture (see Frei, *The Eclipse of the Biblical Narrative*—New York, Harper & Row, 1966, pp. 2-4). It can be an important resource for a postcritical (not anticritical) reading of Scripture in narrative theology and preaching.

38. You may trace the history of the use of typology in *The Cambridge History of the Bible,* ed. G. W. H. Lampe, 3 vols. (Cambridge: The University Press, 1969).

39. Ibid., vol. 3, p. 26.

40. Reginald Fuller, *What Is Liturgical Preaching?* (London: SCM Press, 1957), p. 48.

41. Northrup Frye, *The Great Code: The Bible and Literature* (London: Ark Paperbacks, 1983), p. 79.

42. Ibid., pp. 80-81.

43. For examples of typology see the end of the Jacob and Moses sermons.

44. C. G. Montefiore, *A Rabbinic Anthology* (London: The Macmillan Co., 1938), p. xvi.

45. Ibid.

46. C. H. Dodd, *The Apostolic Preaching and Its Developments* (Chicago: Willett, Clark & Co., 1937), p. 18.

47. Narrative theology and preaching does have its limits, well argued by Richard Lischer, "The Limits of Story," *Interpretation*, 38 (January 1984), 26-38.

48. Stanley Hauerwas argues that our ethics arise from our story; we are a story-formed community who learn how to behave from our redemption story (note 4). James Sanders speaks of the important polarity in biblical faith, *hagadah* and *halakah,* as *mythos* and *ethos* (*God Has a Story Too,* p. 3); we could translate gospel and law. Both are important. *Halakah* preaching would involve series on the Ten Commandments (but never isolated from Exodus), the Sermon on the Mount (but never isolated from the creation, life, death, and resurrection of Jesus Christ), and the seven deadly sins and seven virtues (but never isolated from the Biblical Story and the church's story). Every sermon need not be narrative in form, but all biblical preaching is narrative in character and fits within the larger Biblical Story.